Library of Social Work

General Editor:
Noel Timms
Professor of Social Work Studies
University of Newcastle upon Tyne

Justice for juveniles

The 1969 Children and Young Persons Act: A case for reform?

Philip Priestley
Denise Fears
Roger Fuller

Routledge & Kegan Paul
London, Henley and Boston

First published in 1977
by Routledge & Kegan Paul Ltd
39 Store Street,
London WC1E 7DD,
Broadway House,
Newton Road,
Henley-on-Thames
Oxon RG9 1EN and
9 Park Street,
Boston, Mass. 02108, USA
Printed in Great Britain by
Redwood Burn Ltd
Trowbridge and Esher

British Library Cataloguing in Publication Data

Priestley, Philip
  Justice for juveniles.—(Library of social
  work).
  1. Juvenile delinquency – England – Wiltshire
  1. Title II. Fears, Denise III. Fuller, Roger
  IV. Series
  364.6   HV9147.W/   77-30153

ISBN 0 7100 8703 9

Contents

Introduction

The Children and Young Persons Act of 1969 is on trial.
It is accused by some magistrates and politicians, on the
one hand, of being 'soft' on juvenile crime which con-
tinues to increase at a rate they find unacceptable.
Child-minded critics complain that on the contrary it
retains too strong a punitive element. Administrators,
for their part, applaud the principles of the Act but
regret the absence of cash to carry them out properly.
Both the Home Office and the Department of Health and
Social Security have carried out internal reviews of the
working of the Act; a Parliamentary Expenditure Committee
has reported on its shortcomings; and political action is
likely whichever party is in power.

The debate so far on these issues has been strong on
opinion and short on facts. This book attempts to
redress that deficit, in part at least, by presenting the
results of a research project which looked at all the
children who were dealt with under the provisions of the
Act in Bristol and Wiltshire during the first three
months of 1972. Its findings are not of course conclus-
ive; they refer to only two geographical areas, neither
of them necessarily typical of any other; to less than
two thousand children; and to a period of time just after
the inception of the Act when procedures may not have
assumed their final forms, and the effects of the Seebohm
re-organization were still being felt.

Nor is the book simply a recitation of the 'facts'.
It is rather an argument about the origins of the Act,
about some of the fundamental assumptions behind it; and
about their translation into practices which have far
reaching consequences for those children and their
families who get caught up in them.

The book concludes with proposals for radical change
of a kind which is likely to please neither the die-hards

nor the liberals, but change that might minimize the
damage we do to children in defence of 'law and order',
'the interests of the child' and other abstractions. The
proposals are not a blue-print and our data would support
different conclusions, but they are offered here as a
reasoned contribution to a discussion which threatens
otherwise to be dominated by sentiment and determined by
expedience.

ACKNOWLEDGMENTS

The work on which this book is based was funded by the
Home Office Research Unit and carried out in the Depart-
ment of Social Administration and Social Work of Bristol
University.
   The research could not have taken place without the
permission and co-operation of the Chief Constables, the
Chairmen of the Juvenile Benches and the Clerks of the
Justices, Directors of Social Services, Chief Probation
Officers and Directors of Education in both Bristol and
Wiltshire and the Chief Superintendent of the Western
Region of the Bristol Transport Police. We were also
greatly helped by many individuals who gave us their time
and made records freely available to us. We are grate-
ful to all of them but wish to emphasize that neither
they nor the Home Office are in any way responsible for
the results of the study or the views expressed in this
book.
   We are also indebted to Neil Hamilton-Smith of the
Edinburgh Regional Computing Centre for all his assistance with our data.
   Successive drafts of this manuscript were typed by
Janet Walton-Masters, Brenda Lalonde and Pat Smith.
Brenda Lalonde also carried out many of the interviews
with the sample of practitioners.
   Finally we wish to thank Professor Roy Parker for all
his support and advice throughout the research.
                                    Philip Priestley
                                    Denise Fears
                                    Roger Fuller

Chapter one

Children and the law: 1908-69

The 1908 Children Act, which introduced the idea of a
separate juvenile court jurisdiction, occupies a land-
mark position in the history of child-law in this country.
Its immediate antecedents are easily cited, the passing
of the Probation of Offenders Act in the previous year
and the nine-year-old precedent of the Illinois Juvenile
Court Act.(1) But it is important to look behind the
innovative glitter of its retrospective reputation, to
see it as only one part of an unfolding history, and as
heir to a variety of traditions which have contributed to
the making of English social law.

Historically, common law had acknowledged the special
status of children before the courts in two ways. Below
the age of seven they were deemed incapable of forming
criminal intent and could not be tried at all. Between
the ages of seven and fourteen by the doctrine of 'doli
incapax' the onus was placed on the prosecution to prove
that the child appreciated the wrongfulness of its
behaviour. Beyond that the law made few concessions to
children, either by way of procedure, or in sentencing
practice. Children were liable to be imprisoned, trans-
ported or hanged impartially alongside their convicted
elders. Some students of Anglo-American juvenile law
also point to the mediaeval doctrine of 'parens patriae'
as the origin of an independent legal tradition of concern for children.(2) First enunciated during the reign
of Aethelred the Unready, it permitted the king to inter-
vene in Chancery Court proceedings on behalf of minors
whose interests were not otherwise represented.(3) But
its links with the broad current of child legislation
which began with the Factory Acts of the early nineteenth
century seem tenuous to say the least. This movement
appears to have owed more to the slowly changing concep-
tions of childhood which came to maturity during the

1

seventeenth and eighteenth centuries and which were
expressed in the re-organization of the mediaeval school
curriculum into currently recognizable patterns of age-
graded education.(4)   And of course to the insufferable
exploitation of child labour in the new factories of the
industrial revolution.

There were two important elements in this developing
institutional concern for children, both of them now
reflected in law.   One was concerned with physical abuse,
and the other with moral contamination.   Abuse has been
combated by legal proscription and the progressive regul-
ation of parents' and employers' treatment of children.
Contamination is a more complicated concept with both
negative and positive facets.   Its positive aspect
reveals itself in laws which prescribe and enforce
exposure to the 'wholesome' influences of the educational
system.   Negatively, it grew out of a revulsion at what
went on in the unreformed prisons of the late eighteenth
and early nineteenth century.   James Neild (5), after a
Boxing Day visit to the Bridewell at Shepton Mallet in
1801, gave vent to the contemporary reformist sentiment:

> But it is painful to add, that of the males, young
> beginners in error or in vice, and old offenders, are
> here promiscuously mingled together in perilous assoc-
> iation.   Unruly Apprentices, with Felons of experience
> must surely feel far worse than the mere pressure of
> personal seclusion from the world at large.
>
> Imprisonment is bad enough: But what is this com-
> pared with a daily exposure, amidst evil communica-
> tions, to principles of depravity, and the horrid, the
> almost certain chance of infamy acquired in a recept-
> acle intended for moral reformation!(6)

A thoroughly ambitious and typically mid-Victorian
solution to the joint problems of contamination and
child-neglect was proposed in 1851 by Mary Carpenter, of
Bristol.(7)   Together with Davenport Hill, a judge, she
submitted to Parliament a tri-partite scheme to deal with
what she unsentimentally described as 'the children of
the dangerous and perishing classes'.   This comprised
free day schools for all children; day Industrial Schools
for the neglected, and residential Reformatories for the
criminal.   The last two provisions were to be financed
partly by parental contributions.   Her aim, said Miss
Carpenter, was 'to obtain legislative powers of coercion
over criminal children and for enforcing pecuniary responsibility on their parents'.

The themes of segregation and regeneration which
underlay what Platt has called the Child Saving Movement,
(8) will not be pursued here, except where they lead back

to the creation of the juvenile court. From 1847 onwards
the powers of the courts to send children to prison had
been progressively eroded. At one level, the proposals
for a juvenile jurisdiction simply extended the principle
of child-protection to the operation of justice itself.
'Promiscuous mingling' (9) still took place in the
corridors and waiting rooms of busy court-houses. Hearings held at different times of day in physically separate buildings were designed to avoid the identification
of 'juvenile delinquents' with 'old lags'. But public
appearances in the dock could still brand the child as a
criminal almost as effectively as a stay in the old House
of Correction. The operation of the law itself, in other
words, was recognized as a potentially contaminating
influence. This realization, and the attempts to come to
terms with it, have supplied the agenda for one strand of
the child-law reform movement which persists into the
present time. In 1908 it led to two fundamental departures from the pre-existing criminal law.
     First it introduced privacy by barring public access
to juvenile proceedings. The implications of this will
be looked at later, but the change was not made without
protest.(10) The second, and more important structural
change, was the definition of an age-based criminal jurisdiction in which separate, private and simplified proceedings might apply. At that stage the argument was not
about criminal responsibility as such. There was no move,
for example, to raise from seven the minimum age at which
children could be tried for offences. It centred rather
on the question of public accountability for criminal
acts. And it sought to establish a period during which
children would be shielded from the full consequences of
what they had done, even though they may have acted with
full knowledge of the wrongfulness of their act; even if,
in legal language 'mens rea', or criminal intent, was
demonstrably present. The critical question then was
rather: 'at what age shall this protection cease?'
     The 1908 Children Act set the upper limit at sixteen;
a generous provision at a time when school-leaving age
was not yet universally fourteen. It thus defined a
jurisdiction within which the criminal law still ran in
its entirety, but within which the full impact of
judicial proceedings on the individual offender was subject to considerable mitigation. If the period from
birth to seven years was looked on as one of moral absol-
ution, the ensuing nine years from seven to sixteen
could best be characterized as a kind of 'moral quarantine'. It took the form of a legally structured space
in which the child may be held apart, not as one in whom

some disease is frank, but in whom it is latent. A case
can be made for locating the origins of such a period of
diminished accountability in the notion of 'doli incapax'.
But the construction of the 'moral quarantine' rests on
wider foundations than an easily rebutted presumption of
irresponsibility. It also represents the flowering of a
child-protection impulse based on principles which have
less to do with curing an affliction than with limiting
its spread. It was a remedy that pre-dated any possible
influence by the late nineteenth century positivist
school of criminology. And it was cast in a form, with
arbitrarily drawn lower and upper age limits, that was to
make it a tempting target for later generations of
reformers.

Other, more pragmatic influences were also at work to
influence the 1908 measure; forces which have influenced
similar Acts both before and since. One of the most
well-worn routes to new social law is that which is sign-
posted by official inquiries and commissions. Sometimes
these are set up to satisfy appreciable shifts in public
opinion; some have helped bring order to hopelessly
tangled administrative areas, and some have looked into
scandals. Others have been used as politically expedient
reasons for inaction; and the results of all of them have
been subjected to the hazards of the political process.
The statutory outcomes of such proceedings, as might be
expected, tend to be piecemeal, incremental and lacking
in 'theoretical' coherence. The 1908 Act was no exception to this 'wonderbag' principle of construction for
it consolidated twenty-six previous statutes, before
moving on to break new ground. And contemporary public
discussion and Commons debates of the Bill reveal no
overriding pre-occupation with what we now think of as
the epoch-making idea of separate courts for juveniles.
When Herbert Samuel (11) introduced the Second Reading
he gave as much, if not more prominence, to the penalties
proposed for mothers who overlay their infants in bed,
and for parents who left children unattended in the
presence of lighted fires, as well as to the powers given
to park-keepers to stop and search juveniles on suspicion
of carrying tobacco.(12)

Taken as a whole however the 1908 measure gave impetus
to a process which had first begun with the Factory Acts;
the convergence of law and welfare. To begin with, the
law had simply intervened in the affairs of employers and
parents by creating criminal offences out of behaviour
thought damaging to children. The next step was the
establishment of special institutions for children who
were required to attend them under threat of legal

sanction. Finally, the courts themselves emerged as a species of welfare agency in their own right; ministering to the age-entities they had captured in the net of the 'moral quarantine'. But from its inception, the public-health style of philosophy of the structure was qualified by an assertion, derived originally from 'scientific' theorizing, but rapidly blessed with the irrefutable status of professional common knowledge, which is that children who commit offences possess, if not identical, at least very similar life histories to those who are neglected by their parents.

The Industrial Schools and Reformatory systems that sprang from Mary Carpenter's work had scrupulously preserved both a moral distinction and a physical separation between the two classes. But by 1932 when a new Children Act was before Parliament, it was possible for the Home Office Under Secretary of State, Oliver Stanley (13), to propose the amalgamation of Industrial Schools and Reformatories in this way:

> I know that some people feel that it is unwise and perhaps unfair to mix up in the same school those who are there for punishment for an offence and those who are there for their own protection - that it means that the poor neglected child is contaminated by the bad young offender.(14)

His answer to his own rhetorical challenge was as neat as it was unsubstantiated: 'The fact is that the distinction between the two is largely accidental. The neglected child may only just have been lucky enough not to have been caught in an offence.'

The importance of this attempt to fuse the originally separated groups of the unlawful and the uncared for, was that it led to attempts to raise the minimum age of responsibility to a point at which it was 'fair' to treat children as culpable, and to moves to replace ideas of penalty or punishment with those of education and treatment.

Neglected or abused children are objects of concern and sympathy. Their plight excites pity in the public imagination. Young thieves, on the other hand, arouse anger and indignation which is expressed in demands for punishment and deterrent sentences. Succeeding relays of reformers have sought so to change the labels attached to their charges that increasing proportions of offending children can be brought under the umbrella of neglect and deprivation, where they might be sheltered from the ill-wind of public reprobation. Empirical support for this conceptual prestidigitation is, however, slight. As the number of criminal prosecutions of eight- and nine-year-

old children has declined, for example, there has been
no corresponding increase in care proceedings for children of the same age. Which suggests that, legally
speaking, the two categories are not all that inter-
changeable.

But evidence was superfluous in 1932 since support for
the Bill was so widespread that its passage through the
House was almost totally uncontroversial. Apart, that
is, from some muted criticism concerning the establishment of Observation Centres. Much of the Bill rested on
the work of the Departmental Committee on Young Offenders
which had reported in 1927.(15) It too had come to the
conclusion that there was 'little or no difference in
character and needs between the neglected and the delinquent child'. Accordingly it recommended, and the Bill
provided for, the abolition of distinctions between
Industrial Schools and Reformatories. But aware, perhaps,
of the contradictions on which this confusion of categories threatened to impale them, its authors not only
made continuing provision for separate 'care' proceedings
but they also suggested the establishment of a network of
observation and assessment centres. These might have
permitted, amongst other things, some post-sentence
sorting out of children into sheep and goats, so as to
avoid the melancholy and much feared consequences of
'promiscuous mingling' in the newly designated Approved
Schools. The National Government accepted the first part
of the argument, but declined to implement the second,
presumably because of the 'economic situation' to which
references were made during the Commons Debate. The idea
of classification, however, has lingered on, and is
ritually re-affirmed from time to time, although the
resources to make it a reality somehow fail to material-
ize.

When the 1933 measures finally became law, the pattern
of legal provision for 'children in trouble' assumed the
basic shape it was to retain virtually unchanged until
the 1969 Children and Young Persons Act.(16) Although
procedures and dispositions had been unified to some
extent, there were within it still three distinct jurisdictions, crime, care and truancy, each resting on separate bodies of substantive and case law. Juvenile court
proceedings themselves had been separated physically from
the adult courts, or were time-tabled to avoid any possibility of overlap between the two clienteles. Special
magistrates were chosen to man the juvenile panel; simplified procedures were adopted; the public was excluded
from the room; and the press forbidden to publish names.
Even the words 'conviction' and 'sentence' were no longer

be used in relation to juvenile offenders. Through
these changes rang the injunction to have regard
above all else 'to the welfare of the child or young
person'.

In criminal matters the juvenile courts still had
available to them most of the penalties of the adult
court, apart that is, from imprisonment. They could use
the services of the probation officers. And they could
commit especially troublesome children, first to the
Reformatories and later to the Approved Schools, still
managed by the voluntary bodies which had created and
maintained them from the 1830s onwards. They could not,
however, take a juvenile offender away from home for
offences which would not, in an adult case, attract a
sentence of imprisonment. But apart from these differences of procedure and sentencing the court was, and
still is, basically a criminal jurisdiction. There were
no offences specific to children and it was the job of
the police to enforce the criminal law and to bring the
culprits to book regardless of age, beyond the minimum
age of responsibility.

Criminal law is more interested in particular acts
than in people. It defines crimes in precise detail and
permits consideration of personal elements to enter only
at the sentencing stage. The care and truancy jurisdictions by contrast were designed to bring within the ambit
of the law strikingly broad areas of child behaviour and
experience.

According to the 1933 Act a child or young person in
need of 'care and protection' is one 'who, having no
parent or guardian or a parent or guardian unfit to
exercise care and guardianship or not exercising proper
care and guardianship, is either falling into bad
associations, or exposed to moral danger, or beyond
control....'(17)

A further list specifies children who are themselves
the subjects of sexual or violent offences or who live in
households where such offences have been committed.

The breadth of the definitions, however, has never
generated the same volume of cases as similar jurisdictions in the USA. There, 'care' cases outnumber 'crime'
by sizeable ratios.

In the more legalistic English system, it does not
require a draftsman's eye to recognize the imprecise
nature of the 'care' definitions, nor a lawyer's to
appreciate why so few proceedings have actually been
brought to court beneath their banner. Laying aside the
sex and violence cases, the difficulties of furnishing
proof about the quality of parental care or a child's bad

associations are self-evident.

It is also clear why 'moral danger' became
ively well-used category since it can be tied to a
specific behavioural event in the life of a girl not yet
sixteen, i.e., an act of intercourse or evidence of
circumstances from which its occurrence can be irresist-
ibly concluded. Moral danger is also the ultimate
extension of child-protection; the protection of the
child from him or herself. Lack of proper care is
equally easy to prove when there is evidence of physical
abuse. It is possible that the paucity of care proceedings up to 1971 was due to the self-limiting reluc-
tance of local authorities, the NSPCC, lawyers and
courts to initiate proceedings leading to the possible
imposition of such measures as committal to an approved
school, in what remained a purely civil jurisdiction.
The need for the care measures themselves was not in
doubt, but the grounds for action were difficult to pin
down. In criminal cases just the opposite was true; the
offences provided nicely convenient grounds for action,
but there was growing dissatisfaction with the potentially uncaring nature of some of the sentences and of the
procedures which preceded them.

The Ingleby Committee was appointed in October 1956,
with wide terms of reference which allowed it to examine
some of these contradictions. After reviewing the devel-
opmental history of the juvenile court, the committee's
report, (18) published in October 1960, came to the conclusion that 'the combined effect of these changes has
been to produce a jurisdiction that rests, at least in
appearance, on principles that are hardly consistent.'
These were the necessity of sitting as a criminal jurisdiction at one instant, trying cases according to the
rules of evidence, and 'the requirement to have regard to
the welfare of the child' at the next.

It is not easy to see (the report continued) how the
two principles can be reconciled: criminal responsibility is focused on an allegation about some particular act isolated from the character and needs of the
defendant, whereas welfare depends on a complex of
personal, family and social considerations.

Nor is it easy, after the report's excellent discussion of the dilemma, to reconcile its ensuing 'as-you
were' conclusions with the reasoning that preceded them.
The report had distilled the heart of the matter into
one succinct sentence: 'The weakness of the present
system is that a juvenile court often appears to be
trying a case on one particular ground and then to be
dealing with the child on some quite different ground.'

The solution to this problem which Ingleby clearly
envisaged was to abolish the criminal jurisdiction altogether and to make the commission of an offence simply
one additional ground for care proceedings of the type
defined by the 1933 Act. But the committee, mindful no
doubt of public opinion, and the limits it implied for
what was politically practicable, appeared to draw back
from where its logic had led. Instead of advocating the
abolition of criminal courts for children and young
persons, it proposed the raising of the age of criminal
responsibility to twelve years. Below that, only civil
proceedings were to be possible, even for children who
had committed offences. In the event, the subsequent
1963 Children and Young Persons Act raised the age of
responsibility to ten but did little to further the con-
solidation of the juvenile courts' crime and care jurisdictions. The most outstanding feature of the Act was
its implementation of Ingleby's other main recommendation
which authorized local authorities to undertake preventive work with families at risk.

Not surprisingly this somewhat makeshift measure
failed to stem a rising groundswell of pressure for
reform.

The period before and immediately following the
passing of the 1963 Act was one filled with activities of
considerable importance to child-law. The Kilbrandon
Committee had been sitting since May 1961

to consider the provisions of the law of Scotland
relating to the treatment of juvenile delinquents and
juveniles in need of care or protection or beyond
parental control, and in particular the constitution,
powers and procedure of the courts dealing with such
juveniles ...

It reported in April 1964.(19) In December 1963 the
Labour Party had set up a study group under the chairman-
ship of Lord Longford which published its findings and
recommendations in June 1964.(20)

Kilbrandon reported first and recommended what Ingleby
had not, the abolition of the criminal jurisdiction for
juveniles and its replacement by an interlocking system
of reporters; the equivalents of procurators fiscal;
juvenile panels conducting non-judicial 'hearings'; and a
social education department administered by local education authorities. In contrast to the English situation
it was the extremely under-developed state of Scottish
juvenile justice and child welfare and the unified central
control in the Scottish Office over these areas that made
possible such root-and-branch proposals. Although juvenile courts were allowed under Scottish law, they were not

mandatory, and had been established in only a handful of
places. Elsewhere children had continued to be tried in
the sheriffs' courts.

'The object of these changes', according to Kilbrandon,
'must be, so far as this can be achieved by public action,
the reduction and ideally the elimination of delinquency.'
The classical criminal law was essentially reactive in
character. Kilbrandon's ambition reveals how far the
idea of a juvenile jurisdiction had moved from its
origins and suggests one of the reasons for it. The
criminal law is an evolved tradition which reconciles
common law, statute and precedent. Child-law is much
more of a consciously constructed mechanism for achieving
explicit social goals such as the provision of minimum
standards of child-care. But although some of the aspirations of the child lobby have been openly formulated and
widely accepted, they have tended to be disconnected
desiderata, each desirable in its own right, but lacking
real linkage to any grand theoretical design. Ingleby
had identified one of the primary dilemmas of juvenile
justice, but done little to resolve it. Kilbrandon pro-
jected a whole new set of provisions which would, if
implemented, have established for the first time the
primacy of the connection between school and the social
response to delinquency. In the event his procedural proposals for reporters and hearings were adopted practically
unchanged, except that the executive arm of the system
was located not in the education sector but in the new
Scottish social work departments.

But whilst Ingleby had provoked no real opposition to
its conclusions, and Kilbrandon achieved most of its
aims, the Longford Committee proposals ran into a wither-
ing cross-fire of criticism which forced the whole thrust
of its proposals profoundly off course.

A number of factors contributed to this violent reac-
tion. First 'Crime - A Challenge To Us All' was not a
balanced Blue Book production from a committee with a
membership carefully composed to reflect a range of interests and opinion in the field. It was a party-political
working party whose overtly political commission was to
produce a report that 'should be based on a long-term
Socialist philosophy and present an idealistic framework
for a constructive policy aimed at the prevention of
crime and the enlightened treatment of offenders with
rehabilitation as its primary objective.' Only second
should it 'provide a programme of practical measures...'

In the event the 'socialist philosophy' was confined
to a preamble called 'Justice with mercy' which consists
of vague allegations that continuing social and economic

inequalities, together with the 'get-rich-quick' values
of the affluent society, are somehow at the root of much
criminal behaviour. The discussion of 'The Child and the
Law' which follows is equally firmly rooted in a conventional liberal-humanism, which betrays no distinctively
socialist approach to the problem.

'Anti-social behaviour in a child', it says, 'may
arise from difficulties at home, from unhappiness at
school, from physical or mental handicaps, or from a
variety of other causes for which the child has no personal responsibility.' In its search for a solution to
the problems thus perceived Lord Longford's committee did
not confine itself to tinkering with the age limits, as
Ingleby had, but suggested instead some basic horizontal
regrouping of legal and social work functions, which
antagonized powerful interests at two levels.

At local authority level they proposed an enlarged
Family Service working in tandem with a new Family Court
to offer aid, support and advice to those children and
parents who were struggling with the various causes of
crime beyond their control. At central government level
they wished to see responsibility for all social work
vested with an expanded Home Office. During the next few
years both the nature of local authority social work and
the question of central responsibility for it were to
become the subjects of continuing debate whose resolution
helped to shape the final form of the 1969 Children and
Young Persons Act.

To understand why the study-group's findings aroused
such strong resistance it is useful to look in more
detail at its deliberations.(21)

Invitations to join the committee were sent out in
December 1963 by Lord Longford and Joan Bourne of the
Transport House research department. The aim was to
advise 'the Labour Party on the recent increase in recorded crime, the present treatment of offenders, and the
new measures, penal or social, required both to assist in
the prevention of crime and to improve and modernise our
penal practices.' Its members included criminologists
T.C.N. Gibbens and Terence Morris, crime-writer C.R.
Hewitt, the Daily Mirror columnist and prison visitor
Xenia Field, MPs Tom Driberg, James MacColl, Charles Royle
and Reginald Prentice, and a number of other people who
were later to hold relevant ministerial posts in the
Labour administration which followed: Lord Gardiner and
F. Elwyn Jones, Lord Chancellor and Attorney General res-
pectively; Anthony Greenwood, Margaret Herbison, Beatrice
Serota and Alice Bacon. The late Leslie Hale, MP, was
also a member of the original committee but declined to

sign the final report because he thought it failed to
deal adequately with the adult penal system. His refusal
was significant because the question of juvenile crime
dominated the work of the committee, and the report had
no discernible impact on policy relating to older
offenders.

The major issues which the committee set itself to
study included the departmental authority of the Home
Office, and the strengthening of Section One of the 1963
Children Act, which encouraged preventive work with
families 'at risk'.

Some lesser questions were also asked in the first
document circulated to members, e.g.:

'Should the age of criminal responsibility correspond
to school-leaving age?'

'Should juvenile courts be transformed into Family
Courts?'

'Should Youth Courts be set up to deal with offenders
under 21?'

After twenty-five full meetings, evidence from twenty-
six organizations, and forty-three individuals, plus
visits to various penal establishments, the committee
endorsed, without change, every one of these 'preliminary
questions'.

The question of central control and where it should be
located did not detain the committee long. Terence
Morris presented a memorandum to its first meeting
arguing for a policy of 'administrative integration ... a
number of disparate activities must be brought into a
common plan'. He suggested 'a completely new department
to be called possibly the Department of Corrections and
Social Welfare'. The committee agreed with the principle
of integration but rejected his new name for the Home
Office.

Agreement was also quickly reached that children
should not be exposed to criminal proceedings. Lady
Wootton said in her evidence

Juvenile courts are the wrong way of dealing with them,
for three reasons:
1. the legal setting,
2. the fact that children have to be paraded
   before strangers, and
3. dealing with children in a separate place, for a
   separate purpose, puts them immediately into the
   atmosphere of a delinquent community.

Evidence from the Police Federation also lent support to
these notions and urged the abolition of the juvenile
courts.

The principle of sparing children from the full weight

of the criminal law was not new. The problem that now faced the working party was where to pitch the age of responsibility. Ingleby and the 1963 Act had raised it from eight to ten. Longford and his fellow members made a bid to raise it to the school-leaving age; then fifteen.

'The idea behind this', explained Howard Jones, in a written submission, 'is that we should accept that school children are still being formed by their education rather than the enforcement of personal responsibility through punishment or penal treatment.'

School-leaving age is an attractive place to fix a legal limit, but like any arbitrary division its adoption poses practical problems, which the committee had clearly not thought through. In the first place school-leaving age is a minimum age and the trend throughout the 1950s and 1960s had been towards increasing numbers of children staying on at school voluntarily after fifteen. The argument for treating employed school leavers as adults would apply therefore to a diminishing proportion of children. And moving the age of responsibility from ten to fifteen entailed the crossing of two other kinds of biographical Rubicon; a biological one at puberty, and the criminal one of peak delinquency at age fourteen. In both these respects a fourteen- to fifteen-year-old youth, sexually mature, physically large and criminally experienced, is qualitatively different from the ten-year-old, and unlikely to command the same kind of protective sympathy from the general public.

The only dissenting voices to be heard by the Longford committee against raising the age of responsibility were those of witnesses Otto Shaw and R. Leach, both heads of approved schools, and who did not favour any move above the age of twelve. And only one member of the committee itself raised objections to the powers which the new system would give to the proposed Family Service and Family Court. James MacColl, MP, expressed fears about 'the authoritarian temptations of the professional social worker. There is a danger that these reforms may become tainted by the tyranny of the do-gooders.'

Despite these words of caution the final report of the committee expressed its wish to see an end to the juvenile court, and a substantial shift of power to a social work agency, on the grounds that 'children should receive the kind of treatment they need without any stigma or any association with the penal system'. Appearances in court, even the juvenile one, were thought to mark a possible 'first step towards a criminal career'. The erring child, therefore, was to be referred by the school, or the police, or the parents, to a Family Service in the

first instance. Drawing on a hypothetically ideal range
of facilities and services, the social workers there
would attempt to work out an agreed programme of help,
care or intervention. Failing agreement, the case could
be referred to the Family Court for arbitration. Children referred to the Court were to be dealt with by 'civil
procedure', and removal from home was to be by Fit
Person Order only.

But when the actual detail of this progression was
spelled out, it proved difficult to maintain the neat
coincidence of the age of responsibility with the school-
leaving age. The public protection function of law had
to be recognized in the proviso that 'serious and persistent' offenders under that age could be brought to court
as being 'in need of care or protection'. And the child
protection principle had to be extended beyond that age,
so that fifteen- to eighteen-year-olds, many of them
still at school, could also have the benefit of voluntary
arrangements or, in cases of persistence or seriousness,
criminal proceedings were to be possible for this age
group. These would take place either in the juvenile
court or in the youth court, which was to be set up to
cater for young people between seventeen and twenty-one.

The Longford Committee had been set up to see to the
dissolution of the juvenile courts. It proposed to
achieve this by raising the age of responsibility to sixteen, and fusing the crime jurisdiction of the court into
a new unified care scheme. But like its predecessors,
the plan failed to achieve a neat boundary at the upper
age limit where it met the adult court. To cope with the
problems of overlap and to ease the abrupt transition
from no-responsibility to full responsibility Longford
had found it necessary to re-introduce the 'moral quarantine', this time to cater for the seventeen- to twenty-
one-year-olds in the youth courts.

The appearance of the Kilbrandon report in April 1964
came too late to influence the Longford Committee's conclusions which were published two months later.

Within six months, there was a Labour administration
and those parts of 'Crime - A Challenge To Us All' which
dealt with children became not just tentative proposals,
but Government policy.

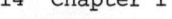 'My Government', said the Queen, when she opened the
new Parliament in 1964, 'will be actively concerned to
make more effective the means of sustaining the family
and of preventing and treating delinquency.'

Alice Bacon, now Under Secretary of State at the Home
Office, produced a White Paper which appeared as 'The
Child, the Family and the Young Offender' in August 1965.

(22)   Faithful to the findings of the Longford group, the introduction to the White Paper claims that 'It is at least clear that much delinquency - and indeed many other social problems - can be traced back to inadequacy or breakdown in the family. The right place to begin therefore,' it argued, 'is with the family.'

A new concept was then introduced, the family council, consisting of '... social workers of the children's service and other persons selected for their understanding and experience of children ...' This was a more precise mechanism than that envisaged in Longford where parents and social workers were to be encouraged to arrive at voluntary agreements outside of any institutional framework.

Whilst the new councils would not possess the power to pass sentences, it was proposed in the White Paper to allow them to direct that children be removed to remand homes for specified short periods of assessment. Other changes simplified the complicated age structure of the Longford proposals from four categories to two: children up to the age of fifteen, and those aged sixteen to twenty-one. And the treatment options available to the family council, the family court and the young offender's court were specified in more detail.

Compared with the system prevailing after the Children and Young Persons Act 1963, the first White Paper depicted a more elaborated model with two distinct power centres, the Family Council and the Family Court, and an attenuated notion of responsibility. Its publication provoked a storm of opposition from magistrates, who resented the abolition of the juvenile court, and from the probation service. One of the main planks in both their platforms was the need to retain judicial forms for making decisions which affected individual liberty.

In its observations on the White Paper, the National Association of Probation Officers reiterated its 'frequently expressed' opinion that

no action should be taken to interfere with the liberty of an individual on grounds of his conduct, or with the rights of parents on allegations of their failings except as the result of a judicial assessment of the fact or allegations which have been regarded as justifying such action.(23)

In its concluding paragraph the memorandum made 'a strong plea that this legislation should not be regarded as a party matter.' A vain hope as later events were to prove.

As the debate over the first White Paper continued it became clear that speedy legislation to implement the Longford vision was no longer possible. Alice Bacon left

her post at the Home Office in August 1967 and the whole
project seemed to lose the impetus it had derived from
her personal involvement.

A second White Paper, 'Children in Trouble', appeared
in April 1968.(24)   In deference to the opposition provoked by its predecessor, it retained the juvenile court
as the principal mechanism for dealing with children who
presented particularly difficult problems of behaviour or
adjustment.   However, the court was to be construed as a
place of last resort, and a number of obstacles were
placed in the way of children ever arriving there.   Co-
operation between police and social workers was to be
'encouraged' along with greater use of police cautions
and liaison schemes.   In formal terms it was proposed that
criminal proceedings against most children would be
brought under the provisions of a new care definition.
This included the commission of an offence as one of the
conditions which, together with the absence of 'such care,
protection and guidance as a good parent may reasonably
be expected to give', could be used to justify a court
case.   Below the age of ten only care proceedings based
on care criteria were to be possible.   The 'offence condition' formula was to apply between the ages of ten and
thirteen.   From thirteen to seventeen a complicated
system of mandatory consultation between police and local
authority social service departments, plus applications
to an examining magistrate, were to be introduced to
ensure that only the most serious offenders were prosecuted, and then only after all other possible approaches
had been tried.

The result was an unhappy compromise between the radical Longford plan and the position of its critics, and
it satisfied neither faction.   It formed, none the less,
the basis of the draft Bill.   Only the examining magistrates disappeared before the Bill came before the
Commons.

The then Home Secretary, James Callaghan, introduced
the Commons second reading of the Bill.   'Its aim', he
said, 'is to protect the deprived and delinquent children
of today from becoming the deprived, inadequate, unstable
or criminal citizens of tomorrow.'(25).   In the Lords,
Lord Stonham elaborated further the purpose of the
measure.

> For many years I have worked on behalf of prisoners,
> the dropouts of a defective society.   Always in
> working with them I have recognized that I am dealing
> with the sorry end product of continuous social fail-
> ure; a combined failure of the machine, the courts and
> of society at large.   With nearly all of them we are

starting too late. This Bill seeks to remedy that, to
deal with the problems at the very beginning.(26)

For the first time in the history of major child legislation in this country the Bill attracted an official
opposition amendment. It was moved by Quintin Hogg, who
thought that it was 'A Bill proposed without adequate
preparation or consultation and open to serious objection
in that it is unjust as between different children in like
case...' The debate in both Houses was preoccupied with
the question of whether deprived and depraved children
were basically the same population. Viscount St David put
the extreme case for the proposition. 'We are not really
concerned with the offences,' he said, 'we are concerned
with the children, and I want to split the two matters
entirely apart.' In the Commons on the other hand,
Emlyn Hooson asserted that 'there is a difference between
a delinquent and a deprived child. A deprived child may
well prove to be a delinquent child but a delinquent child
is not necessarily a deprived child. It is a vitally
important distinction between two types of children.'
Despite these doubts, and the opposition amendment, the
Bill passed virtually unchanged into law as the Children
and Young Persons Act 1969.

But before the law could be implemented the political
process intervened with a change of government in 1970.
Because, like its precursors, the Act consolidated previous measures it was not practicable simply to shelve it
in anticipation of some alternative being introduced.
Instead, the Conservative administration decided to draw
the teeth of the Act by declining to implement the vital
Sections 4 and 5, which allowed for the raising of the
age of responsibility and restricted the prosecution of
older children. It dealt a final blow to the aspirations
of the child lobby and, coupled with the outcome of the
Seebohm Committee's work, (27) set the scene for a new
chapter in the history of children and the law.

Chapter two

Justice and welfare: The elements of a system

The chequered history of the 1969 legislation illustrates some of the obstacles which were encountered in putting into practice the apparently simple intentions of some single-minded reformers. In the event, reality had refused to conform with the ambitious blue-print drawn up by the Longford committee. A switch-back progression of proposals and counter proposals, compounded by the political equivalent of a game of musical chairs, had bequeathed to those charged with implementing the Act a problematical, two-part legacy. The 'letter of the law' is the first part of this duality and it defines what must occur when the legal process is invoked. The 'spirit of the Act', which accompanies it, is a subtler set of hopes and expectations to do with keeping children out of the legal and penal systems, by all means possible. They are complementary and inter-dependent aspects of the same structure; the one providing a hard outline of legal rules; the other breathing life into the dead lines of the statute. And together they form a framework for scrutinizing some relevant features of the arrangements which they authorize.

First there are the formal aims of the Act as passed, which can be summarized as follows:

1. To condense a wide range of pre-existing child law into a single jurisdiction dealing in similar ways with children who: commit offences; stay away from school; or who are in need of care or protection.

2. To establish procedures linking police and social services departments, and permitting the latter to exert some influence over the choice of children to be brought to court, and to help reduce their numbers.

3. To give additional powers to social services departments to play a larger part in 'treatment', and to

> determine the meaning of court-made 'care orders'
> according to their own interpretations of a child's
> needs.

Implementation of the Act left intact only the last of
these items, namely the enlargement of social work power
over children placed in care. Combined dispositions for
crime and care proceedings, in the form of the new supervision and care orders, had widened the range of cases,
and deepened the treatment options open to the social
services departments. But the pursuit of a totally
integrated crime-care system was obstructed by the reten-
tion of criminal proceedings. The elegantly drafted
common criteria for bringing children under fourteen to
court now became in practice the grounds for bringing
care and truancy cases only. And so much damage had been
done to the 'spirit of the Act' by tampering with the
'law's letters' that a restatement of the underlying
philosophy had to be issued in the shape of 'A Guide for
Courts and Practitioners'.(1) This re-emphasized that
the purpose of the legislation was to avoid juvenile
court appearances, and stressed the use of police cautions
as a prime means of achieving this. What the law no
longer sanctioned, in other words, was to be achieved by
exhortation.

As a charter for a new welfare dispensation, the Act
was therefore, by the time of its due date, a pretty
broken-backed affair. The attempted coup against the
criminal stigmatizing of children had failed, and the new
order, like the old, reflected deep divisions in both
professional and secular opinion over the right approach
to the problems of juveniles. These divisions derive
largely from the dialectic between the demands of justice
on the one hand, and of welfare on the other, which has
informed the continuing debate about how to deal with
children in trouble. The age-related 'moral quarantine'
of the juvenile court jurisdiction represents one pain-
fully constructed accommodation between the two positions.
We have already seen something of the difficulties which
attended the fixing of precise lower and upper age limits.
Some of the system's other contradictions can be discussed at the conceptual, the organizational and the
idealogical levels.

CONCEPTUAL

At the heart of the conceptual difficulties is the question of 'equality before the law'; a phrase of almost
infinitely elastic meaning, but one which basically

embodies a notion of 'fairness' in the application of
standard procedures and sentences to particular cases.

Three features of the English criminal law are com-
monly held to safeguard its even-handed practice. The
first is the advocacy principle of trial; the second is
the public nature of the proceedings; and the third is
the right of appeal against both conviction and sentence.
All three have been subtly but insistently undermined
during the drift from justice to welfare that has characterized the development of juvenile justice both in
Europe and North America from the end of the nineteenth
century onwards. In the British Isles traces of three
distinct stages in this process exist side by side. In
Eire the provisions of the 1908 Act are still in evidence. In England and Wales there is a mixed justice/
welfare system typical of many other countries. And
Scotland has adopted 'hearings' under the 1968 Social
Work Scotland Act which does away with the strictly legal
setting altogether. The motive power of this movement
has been provided by a set of determinist beliefs about
the causes of anti-social behaviour in children and its
identification with child abuse and neglect. Both conditions have been ascribed to factors outside the control
of the afflicted children who must, as a consequence, be
regarded as not responsible for them. An adversarial
system of justice can only operate on the basis of
assumed personal responsibility for behaviour. It is no
accident therefore that where the notion of irresponsibility has made most progress, there also has the practice
of trial by due process fallen most into disuse. In
Norway which removed children completely from the reach
of the criminal law as early as 1896,(2) and in other
Scandinavian countries, cases are heard by Welfare Boards
whose deliberations in some cases have so far departed
from the legal model as to no longer require even the
presence of the relevant child.(3) In the USA and
England and Wales, where the judicial form has been retained, the advocacy principle has still withered into
various stages of desuetude.

It is true that in summary justice for adults as well
as for juveniles the guilty plea is more typical than the
contested case. But the absence of skilled defence
representatives must have contributed to the progressive
attrition of the trial-like nature of the proceedings.
That apparently is exactly what happened in the USA where
sloppy judicial practice involving denials of the basic
legal rights of the accused continued unchecked until the
Gault (4) decision shook a cold shower over the uncrit-
ical acceptance that all was for the best when all the

parties to court proceedings claimed to be acting 'in the best interests of the child'.

Blinded by a natural but sentimental reverence for such high ideals the child welfare lobby has tended to limit its calls for change to 'more of the same'. Its members may well have applauded in 1908 when the public was barred from the back of the juvenile court room, thus creating what they saw as a desirable inequality before the law, and removing at the same time one of the safe-guards of the trial. And they may even have derived satisfaction from the virtual disappearance of conflict over the decisions which the courts finally reached con-cerning the children before them. Lawyers are not equipped by training or experience to challenge effec-tively anything other than gross errors of fact in the evidence presented by social workers in support of their conclusions. The low rate of appeals against sentence from the juvenile court may be attributed to these inabil-ities, reinforced, perhaps, by the fact that the 'sever-ity' of the decisions is not apparent in advance. The indeterminacy of the care order, like that of the approved school order which preceded it, contains a promise of early release from its conditions. The sev-erity, if it occurs at all, has to be 'earned' during the period of the order by continuing bad behaviour, or is deemed necessary by persistently negative social work assessments of the child's home. Appeals against super-vision or care orders can also be made to appear as contradictory by the superficially benign mould in which they are cast. Conceptually, then, the system is in permanent tension between its judicial and its social work elements.

ORGANIZATIONAL

Organizationally it is little better off. For the purposes of this research we have designated as 'the system' all those activities and institutions which deal with 'children in trouble' within the framework of the 1969 Children and Young Persons Act, together with its associated statutory instruments and Home Office circul-ars. At first sight, the most salient characteristic of this 'system' in action is its episodic nature. In fact the use of the word 'system' to describe such a loosely linked and discontinuous set of arrangements, although a convenient shorthand, is probably misleading.

To the victim of a crime, whose complaint triggers off a majority of police-child encounters, the experience of

detecting and reporting the offence events is something
that takes very little time and seldom leads to any
further involvement in the case. For a police force, the
processing of juvenile cases is a task which absorbs not
more than a few per cent of its total outlay of time,
manpower and other resources. It is not, on that account,
lightly regarded by them, but it remains a less than
central activity whose loss would not make any great
impact on either their work-schedules or their professional self-conceptions. And when their investigations
are completed they present a well-constructed prosecution
case to the court, expressing as they do so a professional
disinterest in the outcome.

Nor does dealing with children in trouble constitute
more than a minor part of the workloads of the other
agencies involved: schools, social services and probation
departments. Schools provide reports on pupils who
appear in court; a procedure which accounts for only a
tiny proportion of their efforts. Preparing social
enquiry reports on juvenile offenders and coping with
those who are allocated to them under supervision orders
is also unlikely to take up more than a fraction of the
notional output of a typical social services department.
(5) And the probation service, which has been tradition-
ally associated with juvenile delinquents, has in recent
years assumed increasing responsibilities for institutional casework and after-care with adults which have
progressively overshadowed the importance and volume of
its work with children.

Only the juvenile court, at the centre of the system,
is wholly and uniquely concerned with children and their
problems. But in some respects it is a qualitatively
different agency from all the others which supply it with
cases and take some of them back for the administration
of 'treatment'. Apart from the clerk, who may serve the
juvenile court alongside his duties in the adult jurisdiction, and an usher or two, the magistrates command no
substantial executive resources to translate their collective will into action. In other ways the principal
figures in the juvenile court are typical of the actors
already considered.

Although the lay status of the bench members sets them
apart, in one crucial respect, from the surrounding
'professional' services, their part-time participation in
the juvenile justice system is of a piece with all the
rest. Not one of its parts consists of a whole-time, or
professional service dedicated exclusively to the problem
in hand. The 'system' then, such as it is, is a patch-
work fabrication woven from the fringes and the margins

of its contributing agencies.

To this state of affairs it is possible to ascribe both costs and benefits. The costs can be counted first in terms of administrative inefficiency. The parcelling up of cases into discontinuous segments, each dealt with by basically uncoordinated agencies, each with their own superordinate and necessarily dissimilar goals, might justifiably be presented as a paradigm of how not to organize a service for children in trouble. Longford and his committee clearly leant towards the simplification of juvenile justice by bringing all the bits together, so far as possible, under one over-arching administration. In the mid 1960s, it was consistent with the temper of the times to argue for administrative rationalization and concentration in the public sector on the grounds that this would prevent the overlapping of services and achieve economies of scale. The re-organisation of local social services, and later of local government itself, are lasting memorials to the power of these arguments. Their application to the juvenile court and its cohorts of agencies was, however, thwarted by the inassimilable and autonomous powers of the police and the magistracy.

The indigestible lump in the bland organization envisaged by the first White Paper thus proved to be the principle of the separation of powers. Justice and welfare had, over the preceding century, become 'promiscuously mingled and mixed' to a degree which earlier jurists would have deemed impossible, but the potency of the remaining legal element now became a sticking point which prevented the complete homogenization of the two elements into one neat whole. As a result, three principal and independent power-centres: police, magistracy and social services, still pool their resources in an ad-hoc system of co-operation which does not disguise the absence of central control over the diversity of its component parts.

On the one hand this diversity assures at the least a possibility that procedures which have been designed to be fair, purposeful and universal will turn out to be capricious, contingent and idiosyncratic. But from the defendant's point of view, diversity whether of conception or of operation can also act as one kind of safeguard against the development of an ideological or organizational hegemony against which all appeal is futile. It may only be the astute or the self-assured or the well-represented who are able at present to exploit these opportunities, but at least they are there.

In another way the consequences of the 1969 Act are of less potential benefit to the children it was designed to

help. The battle of the White Papers had been fought and
drawn, in part over the divorce of decision-making and
executive action. The courts had kept intact the major
part of their criminal jurisdiction over children but
social services had won a wider area of power, particularly in the interpretation of 'care orders'; whilst the
police were being 'encouraged' to extend the practice of
cautioning. The net effect has been the disappearance of
much decision-making behind closed doors.

To many defendants in court, the decisions reached by
the bench may well be made on grounds which remain quite
opaque, but they are generally based on information which
is openly presented and potentially open to challenge.(6)
The final decision can also be appealed to a higher court.
Police and social services decisions, although equally
fateful for the future of the child, are subject to no
such safeguards. Both of these decision-making processes
are inaccessible to the child and his family, or their
representatives.

Given such organizational defects, the most pertinent
question might not be 'how well does this system work?'
as much as 'how does it work at all?' Despite continuing
criticisms from police and court quarters, the fact is
that it manifestly does work on a day-to-day basis. That
it does so may be an unexpected tribute to the unsuspec-
ted possibilities of running, without centralized control
of any kind, systems involving an intricate inter-agency
orchestration of events and processes. To many politicians and to chief officers of social services departments, consultation, co-ordination and collaboration are
poor substitutes for a unified administration, but the
sovereignty of the subscribing authorities which they
head seems unlikely to yield in the near future to any
further essays in amalgamation.

IDEOLOGICAL

In the absence of clearly chartered objectives and of a
unified administration, what is it that provides drive
and direction to the system we are describing? In one
sense the real thread of continuity running through it is
the subjective experience of the children and parents who
are caught up in it. They alone, although excluded from
some critical areas, see the procedures through from
start to finish. But, with rare exceptions, they provide
a mainly passive linkage to the proceedings. A more positive organizing principle may be sought in the attitudes
and beliefs of the key people who man the child-law

system: the police, social services and probation
officers, and juvenile court magistrates. Whilst they
must all operate within the 'letter of the law' there is
considerable scope for the expression of departmental
policies and personal or professional philosophies within
the 'spirit of the Act'. It was in order to gain some
idea of what these views were, in Bristol and Wiltshire,
that interviews were conducted with sixty-six selected
practitioners. They comprised all the chairmen of the
juvenile benches; all the juvenile bureau officers in
Bristol; senior policemen in each divisional headquarters in Wiltshire; together with randomly chosen
social workers, fourteen in Wiltshire and twelve in
Bristol; and seven probation officers in each area.

They agreed that the 1969 Children and Young Persons
Act was designed to do two related things. First, it was
thought to be concerned with avoiding, as far as possible,
the appearances of children in court. And second it was
seen as a vehicle for promoting a shift away from punishment and towards treatment: interpreted in its widest
sense.

A senior policeman said

A very concise explanation would be that it was intended to try and keep juveniles out of court so far as
was reasonably possible. By trying to regard wayward
juveniles perhaps less as criminals and more as
persons who should be assisted to find their own way
in life, and perhaps to reduce the nature of punishment which was awarded to them; if only by a change of
phraseology for places like approved schools, altered
to residential homes.

The bridge between the notion of treatment and that of
punishment is the idea of removing or lessening the
stigma of criminality, although specific mechanisms for
achieving this are not often mentioned. Frequent references are made to the need for more facilities, more
money and greater flexibility, but surprisingly few of
them relate to the actual practice of consultation
between police and social services departments. The few
who do mention it tend to be policemen and, of twenty-one
social workers interviewed, only one spontaneously mentioned consultation as an aim of the Act. This suggests
that at the time the interviews took place consultation
concerning juvenile offenders had made little real impact
on the daily work of social workers in Wiltshire and
Bristol.

A handful of people, magistrates and probation
officers, drew attention to the shifts of power from
themselves to social services which are entailed in the

implementation of the Act. And there were five individuals, representing all the groups except police, who
pleaded ignorance of the Act and its provisions. A few
others thought the purpose of the Act was to consolidate,
tidy up and extend previous child legislation.

The emphasis in most of these responses on the 'spirit'
of the Act was expressed by one social worker who saw it:
'as a mood rather than a specific, down the line policy.
A mood rather than a guideline. A mood to consider the
family as a unit within the community.'

But within this mood, as caught and interpreted by
social workers, there are marked differences of interpretation from:

'To give social services more subtlety of control over
people - for their own good.'

to:

'To treat rather than punish the behaviour of children
who break the law. Seeing children and behaviour as a
response to pressures ...'

and:

'The word "treatment" I dislike because it comes down
to classic individualism ... It is no accident that
the type of children I come across in care are working-
class kids from working-class areas. We are trying to
get away from formal judicial practice and giving
people who have some theories, at least, about social
behaviour, more latitude to help them.'

The first is frank, if a little disturbing; the second
represents mainstream thinking in all the practitioner
groups; whilst the third may well stem from recent
training in which 'social factors' and 'labelling'
theories were dispensed.

Support for the perceived aims of the Act was over-
whelmingly evident. Only one person, a magistrate,
actually expressed dissent, and a further fifteen out of
the sixty-six gave general support but with minor reservations. The magistrate who objected thought that:

The intention was rather good - and extremely sloppy.
I think they were after consoling the children and
trying not to make them feel unacceptable, and trying
to remove any power around them which might restrain
their natural development.

She suspected the motives of 'a government who were keen
on getting votes at that point', and concluded 'I don't
think it was wholly with the interests of the child at
heart'.

The fact that every other magistrate interviewed, that
is every juvenile chairman in two court areas, agreed
with the aims of the Act suggests that the criticisms

sometimes retailed by the Press are not wholly typical.

Despite widespread goodwill towards the Act, there persists amongst the practitioners a feeling that the
intentions of its authors are being frustrated by a lack
of facilities, of funds, of residential places and of
skilled workers. And by the self-defeating leniency, as
some of them saw it, of the treatment being meted out to
older, less impressionable offenders who tended to construe it as weakness. The lack of resources was felt
with particular keenness by social workers, although
there is an interesting divergence between Wiltshire and
Bristol in this respect. All but one of the Wiltshire
social workers say that the Act is not working too well.
More than half the Bristol workers, on the other hand,
either agree with or give qualified support to the idea
that things are working out. It is possible that the
difference is due to the existence of a police juvenile
bureau in Bristol, whose officers actively seek contact
with any social worker thought to be involved with a
juvenile coming to their notice.

Members of the four actor groups suggest a range of
reasons for the failure fully to implement the Act. The
problem of defining success exercised one policeman:

> If the child we deal with at the age of eight keeps
> out of trouble until he's eighteen, is that success-
> ful? On the other hand if the child you deal with
> leniently at the age of fourteen commits another
> offence at fourteen and a half is that failure? You
> can't turn a Hell's Angel into a choir-boy purely and
> simply by making a decision to deal with him leniently
> or to take him before a court.

A policeman and a probation officer were critical of
the length of time it now took to get children to court,
a hiatus caused, paradoxically they thought, by the very
consultation procedures which were designed to serve the
best interests of the children. The lack of sanctions in
the cases of children already in care who committed
further offences concerned a magistrate and a policeman.
And the sense of losing control over the subsequent
career of a care case weighed particularly heavily with
some magistrates. In many instances it is the prematur-
ity of the Act's implementation to which these criticisms
revert:

> The whole exercise was set up without qualified staff
> or facilities to implement it. You wouldn't get away
> with it in business but in politics you can.

But both magistrates and police reported a growing
confidence, both in the ability of social services to
improve the level of their service to the courts, and in

the quality of their judgments concerning particular
cases.

The move from punishment to treatment mentioned by
many of those interviewed could be represented as a
simple linear progression. But that would do less than
justice to the subtleties and complexities that relate
the two concepts. Some of these were elucidated when
practitioners were asked to specify kinds of cases where
punishment might be necessary rather than help. This
task caused considerable difficulty, and although certain
types of offence, e.g., violence or vandalism, and particular types of children, e.g., 'deliberate' or
persistent offenders, were most thought to merit punishment, almost half of the people interviewed wished to
explain in greater detail what they meant by the terms
treatment and punishment. There were one or two who
thought that virtually every offence deserved to be
punished in some way, like the Probation Officer who
said: 'I've always believed in punishment to a certain
extent for all those who've done wrong. But', he continued, 'I don't believe in it by itself. It should be
combined with help or other things ...' And there were a
few, all but one of them social workers, who totally
rejected the idea of punishment either in theory or in
practice. 'I've never come across any that needed punitive treatment.'

But it is the qualifying phraseology in the first of
these answers which provides the key to a more prevalent
attitude. The response of the courts and the social
workers, by this view, should be a judicious blend of
censure or penalty on the one hand and sympathetic good
sense on the other. Striking the balance between these
two ingredients is the essence of the art of sentencing.
It is best expressed by a 'craftsman' analogy: the production of results by methods which defy coherent analysis, but which those with the knack 'know' to be right
at the moment of making a decision. At the centre of the
art is the ability to 'individualize' and to do what is
best for 'that' child in 'these' circumstances.

'There are some juveniles that commit the same offence
that require punishment, while others require assistance;
help through the courts', said one policeman, and the
same views were expressed, in different ways, by representatives of the other three groups, social workers,
probation officers and magistrates.

The child's needs are held to be the determining factor in making these decisions, but it is the subjective
meanings of 'help' and 'punishment' which make the whole
issue so problematical. 'What do you mean by punishment?'

asked a magistrate. 'We hope that anything we do is
therapeutic.' This attitude rests partly on a dislike of
the semantic connections of the word 'punishment' and was
strongly put by another JP.

> We all suffer in life. We all make mistakes and are
> punished. If we are sensitive, we feel remorse and
> that is punishment. I'm not sure that punishment is a
> very useful word today. If you talk of punishment
> people either think you're a hard liner, wanting ven-
> geance, or you're a softie who will pat them on the
> head and tell them not to do it again. I'd be happier
> to use the word consequence, 'If you do this, this
> will happen.'

One solution to the problem is for sentencers simply
to re-define all they do as 'treatment', as in 'Punishment can be treatment', or 'Punishment is only a technique
for promoting change', thus effectively squaring the
circle. At the same time, according to a magistrate:

> Punishment as such doesn't help. But one wonders
> where the line is drawn between punishment as punish-
> ment and punishment as help. Some things which might
> be considered by the youngsters as punishment at the
> time could well prove to be helpful.

This introduces the perspective of the child who is being
'treated' or 'punished'. Social workers in particular
were aware that what they might think of as help might
seem to the child to be unmitigated punishment.

> Whether we like it or not most children see care or
> supervision as a punishment. This merely reflects the
> prison system. The number of children I have taken
> into care and the parents say, 'How long has he got to
> do?' It is very difficult to convince a family that
> counselling is help. 'Help' is actual, physical giving
> of clothes, money, holidays or whatever. This is how
> they see help in a positive way.

In other words: 'What we see as help, they see as punishment.'

The very fact of appearing in court is thought by some
to be sufficient punishment for many children; particularly those who display a decent shame at what they have
done and where it has got them. The public aspect, too,
of court proceedings, even those involving juveniles, was
thought important by a few: 'Society has to be appeased.'

It is difficult to draw neat conclusions from such a
richly figured picture, but between those who deny all
utility to the idea of punishment, and those in whose
thinking it still occupies a prominent position, there is
a broad band of opinion where the distinction between
punishment and treatment is blurred to a point where the

two ideas cease to be opposites, or even separate concepts and become instead subsidiary facets of the process
of doing 'what is best for the child'.

One indication of how this position might be trans-
lated into practice was the demand by a small number of
people for 'punishment to fit the crime'. Putting
vandals to clear up the mess, or to dig old ladies' gardens
are particular examples. Significantly perhaps it was the
social workers and magistrates who were most concerned to
emphasize the congruent nature of treatment and punishment, and not the police, who were content in the main to
distinguish violent or persistent offenders as suitable
cases for retribution.

The replies to a number of other questions are also
useful in trying to determine the extent of agreed attitudes amongst system personnel. The first was one which
asked for a list of the characteristics of a 'typical'
juvenile offender. One in four of those interviewed
prefaced their answers to this query with disclaimers to
the effect that no such thing existed as a 'usual' or
'typical' child who gets into trouble.

'I tend to see them as individuals', said one of them,
paraphrasing a common feeling. Many others also experienced obvious difficulty in getting off the ground with
their generalizations. But once started most of them
were able to convey some sort of impression of the child
they normally dealt with; some very briefly:

'A twelve- to fourteen-year-old boy shoplifting in
Woolworths.'

'In the main, council house tenants.'

Others gave more detail although the average typification
contained three items of description only; a surprisingly
parsimonious kind of picture. A full inventory of all
the 'typical' case attributes given by the interviewees
would run to around thirty items, which can be conveniently grouped under the following four heads:

1. Family
2. School
3. Personal
4. Social context

Of these the family emerges as most important in the
minds of most of the practitioner groups. Two thirds of
the 'typical' portraits contain at least one family
factor. Individual and school-related factors form two
smaller but still sizeable groups each receiving men-
tions from approximately half those interviewed. Social
characteristics trail well to the rear in the descriptive
catalogue and feature in only nine of the portraits given
by individual practitioners.

These answers overlapped to a considerable extent
those which were given to the next question which was:
'What do you consider to be some of the most important
causes of juvenile delinquency?' Description spills over
easily into the ascription of causes and the same factors
of home/family, school and personal, and environmental
pressures recur in both accounts; as does a difference in
emphasis between policemen and other practitioners.
Although the numbers involved are small and cannot be
used to support any weighty conclusions it appears that
whilst the social workers, probation officers and magistrates are more likely to stress intra-family and intra-
personal causes of delinquency, the policemen concentrate
on more external matters. The two perspectives are
summarized in these replies from a police officer and a
social worker:

The constable thought that crime arose from:

> The opportunity and the circumstances. I can tell you
> better what I don't believe are the causes of delin-
> quency. I don't go along with this rubbish that it's
> the parents' fault every time because there are a hell
> of a lot of kids where parents couldn't really have
> done much more for them. On the other hand I'm not
> just thinking of material things. There are kids from
> so-called good homes who in fact I would blame the
> parents for. You know the parents have given them
> everything materially but they haven't given them time
> themselves. We find this time and time again. The
> so-called problem families - there's a lot more family
> unity and care and consideration for the kids than
> ever you get in the better class families. What
> happens is that we always wait for the offence and
> then we relate it to the past and try and find some-
> thing that fits.

The riddle of increasing rates of property crime in a
materially affluent society was raised in many of the
other replies even when they start from different premises, as this social worker did:

> One cause is the lack of genuine interest of parents
> for children. This of course is often caused by the
> lack of understanding. They think that affection is
> shown in terms of giving. They are not being good
> parents. It is the easiest way out. They do not like
> to put themselves out to encourage children in useful
> activities. They think that money can pay for every-
> thing.

Whatever their disagreements on the causes of crime
there was one issue which united respondents from all
groups. This concerned what might happen if society were

to do little or nothing about the juvenile offences which
are currently dealt with by the police and social workers
and courts. Most of the practitioners we spoke to had
agreed that the aims of the 1969 Act entailed a move away
from punishment towards treatment and that these were
aims of which they approved. But when they were asked to
envisage a state of affairs where society made little
formal response to the problem of delinquency a rather
different picture emerged. A third of the practitioners
foresaw immediate increases in the rate of crime, both
juvenile and adult. Another third entertained visions of
what they described as 'anarchy'; a world of unbridled
behaviour characterized by private vengeance and vigil-
ante posses. A very few ventured to suggest that there
would be surprisingly little difference in either the
crime rate or the nature of community life. But the
majority response clearly indicates that in the last
resort our policemen, social workers and magistrates saw
themselves as manning a thin blue line between order and
disorder, between civilization and chaos.

It would be wrong merely on the basis of the replies
to these questions to draw more than a tentative infer-
ence, but if one were to be drawn, it would be in the
direction of a division of opinion between policemen and
other practitioners. This division is not a direct conflict of views but a question of relative perspectives.
Policemen appear to emphasize the situational determin-
ants of childish bad behaviour rather than the family
factors stressed by others working in the system. They
also appear to take a more phlegmatic view of punishment,
seeing it as appropriate in certain cases without wishing
to disguise it as anything other than an unpleasant
experience designed to deter rather than reform. On the
basis of these questions it would also be wrong therefore
to conclude that there exists amongst the people who
operate the child-law system, a strong ideological con-
sensus which holds together what ought otherwise to be an
administrative shambles. So far then, this survey of
some of the formal and informal components that go to
make up the 'system' has failed to discover what might
be seen as the vital spark that animates its scattered
elements into concerted action.

One additional clue to the possible identity of such a
dynamic principle may be found in the respectful compli-
ance which marks the demeanour of children and parents
who find themselves in court. This could be due to many
things: the working of guilty minds, simple deference in
the presence of assumed social superiors, or an absence
of social skills sufficient to match the occasion. All

may play their part in particular cases, but all are
secondary in strength and importance to a strongly
socialized attitude in our culture, towards the 'legitim-
acy' of law.   Fear of physical coercion, which ultimately
underpins the whole system, cannot by itself account for
this respect, which is often given, not just freely, but
with apparent gratitude as well.   Nor can it explain the
equal respect which the courts of law inspire in those
who keep them supplied with cases.   Courts cast about
them an aura of priority and urgency which affects all
who come within their orbit.   Their fixed dates exert
enormous influence over time-tabling and work distribution in associated agencies.   Prosecution papers must be
ready; social enquiry reports have to be completed; witnesses and prosecuting officers are required to be in
attendance, at the right time on the appropriate day.

    Courts of course share this attribute with other public
occasions which take place to a pre-arranged time-table.
Teachers organize their work towards an examination date.
Actors are bound by the rigid timing of curtain-up.   But
the court can combine and transcend the demands of time
and place which dominate other settings, through its
function as social drama.   When a court sits, society is
as it were materialized through the medium of the magistracy or the judiciary.   Abstractions like the State or
the Community are made suddenly manifest in full view of
some of their members.   Its effect may be to inspire awe
or provoke fear, but it rarely induces indifference.

    Like other forms of the drama, courts also require
the presence of an audience.   By banning the public from
the back of the court the 1908 Act may have done more to
imperil the survival of the infant juvenile jurisdictions
than all the subsequent efforts of their detractors put
together.   Because without spectators, spectacle may
become empty ritual and procedure pointless rhetoric.
And the justification for law-like procedures is weak-
ened when justice can only be seen to be done at second-
hand through the columns of the local newspaper.

    It can only be a matter for speculation how far factors
of this sort contributed to the fierceness with which
magistrates resisted the reduction of their jurisdiction
which reform of the juvenile court threatened during the
1960s.   What is not in doubt is the fact that magistrates,
although generally successful in the defence of their
court, were forced to cede certain of their powers to the
social services departments.   Social workers too had
gained disappointingly little of what they had been led
to expect.   The police, alone, amongst the major agencies
involved, emerged from the proceedings with fresh powers

they had never solicited. Lord Longford and his committee had sought to reduce the judicial and punitive
components of the system for dealing with children in
trouble.   It is ironic that the eventual outcome of their
work was to strengthen considerably the role of the
police as gate-keepers to the English system of juvenile
justice.

Chapter three

Entering the system: Children coming to the notice of the police

Police forces possess wide and growing powers over the citizens of the industrial states they have been set up to serve. In England and Wales, the countervailing powers of the citizenry over the police, either directly or via their elected representatives, are restricted and ill-defined. The law sets limits to what the police may do, but is silent as to how they shall do it. Restraints on this freedom of action as at present constituted are limited and not necessarily very effective. Parliament may pass laws which the police must enforce, but only in tune with a set of priorities of their own determining. Finance is split fifty-fifty between central and local government, but apart from the direct responsibility of the Home Secretary for the Metropolitan Police, central authority is unable to do much more than use the goads and incentives of inspection and the Exchequer contribution to encourage their adoption. Local control rests nominally with the Police Authority which is appointed by the local authority and equipped with a brief that permits it to advise, but not direct, in matters of peace-keeping and police work.

Justices of the Peace are also the custodians of vestigial powers of police command, which have not been used since before the Police Acts of the early nineteenth century. And there is an additional restriction on local police autonomy in that there exists a list of heterogeneous offences, e.g., incest, murder, inducement to take part in a lottery, which cannot be prosecuted at the discretion of the local force alone, but must first be submitted to the Director of Public Prosecutions for his endorsement.(1)

A number of consequences flow from the administrative detachment of the police. Some of them, such as the internal investigation and adjudication of complaints made by members of the public, are not relevant to this discussion. But the autonomous powers of the police to make decisions concerning the prosecution or not of offenders are of central importance. Their impact is felt, not only in the fateful influence they exert over the lives of individual law-breakers, but also in the shaping and editing of the whole flow of cases which eventually come before the courts.

Within this context of detached power with confused lines of accountability the ordinary police officer faces more immediate problems related to his simultaneous statuses as an Officer of the Crown, sworn to preserve the Queen's Peace, and answerable only in law for his actions in doing so, and as a subordinate officer in a military style organization. The constable on the beat who enjoys theoretical autonomy of action normally assoc-iated with membership of the professions is simultan-eously subject to the kind of discipline that would not disgrace an army. The conflicting demands of autonomy and hierarchy may find expression in a variety of personal and organizational dilemmas. One of them can be seen in the structure of police decision-making.

In the every-day dealings of police departments with suspects and detected persons, there are two points at which discretion can be exercised. The first of them takes place at the boundary of the organization and is concerned with the intake of cases into the police net-work. It is initiated by the registration of complaints from members of the public or by successful routine police work. The officer on the spot must decide for himself whether to arrest or report someone for a crime, or suspected crime, which has come to his attention. More serious offences must be reported; not to do so is a breach of police discipline. The more trivial the offence, however, the more likely it is that the officer will weigh the relative advantages of inaction or infor-mal action, against more formal proceedings. Police discretion of this kind in juvenile cases has been intensively researched and reported in a number of American studies.(2) One of their principal findings is that the demeanour of the youth being questioned has a vital bearing on the outcome of his encounter with the patrol-man. Since our research is based on a study of documentary sources, we have no direct evidence of the part which demeanour plays in the equivalent English sit-uation.

In one case we witnessed in a juvenile court, however, the prosecuting officer related how a constable approached a youth he had seen late at night lying across the

handlebars of a motor-cycle. When asked what he was
doing, the youth replied 'Piss off'. He was arrested and
prosecuted for being drunk in charge of the bike. A
softer answer might well have forestalled the official
wrath that followed, and led to some negotiation about
how he was to get home without breaking the law.

A secondary finding of the studies in the USA was that
the presence at the scene of the crime of a voluble and
irate complainant was significantly associated with high
rates of arrest.(3)   That also lies outside the scope of
our work, but it points to the crucial role of the victim
of a crime, or of the complainant, whose willingness to
report the matter at all is the first of a series of con-
tingencies which between them determine the characteristics of the population that comes to official notice.

Not all crimes, of course, have victims. There are,
for instance, purely reflexive offences, such as posses-
sing cannabis. And others where only a broadly defined
public interest is threatened. Traffic offences form an
important part of the last category and are one example
of what have come to be thought of as breaches of 'regulations' or of 'administrative law'. There are also
offences which can take place only with the co-operation
of the 'victim'; as in unlawful sexual intercourse.
Arrest rates for such offences where there are no
aggrieved victims, and which give rise to few if any
complaints, are clearly functions of police activity.
Self-report studies, on the other hand, record very high
proportions of children questioned who admit to the
commission of criminal acts, many of which have readily
identifiable victims; and most of which remain officially
undetected.(4)   More recent studies of the incidence of
criminal victimization, reveal the obverse face of these
facts; namely a selective reticence on the part of
victims to report certain types of crime.(5)

Rape is a highly under-reported act; and an exception
to the rule that the more serious offences, involving
personal injury or substantial money losses, are generally the most likely kinds of crime to be notified to the
police. Car theft is the only offence which never goes
un-reported. Businesses tend to be more flexible and
often turn a discretionary eye in the direction of
'pilfering' by employees or larcenies from self-service
shops by over-enthusiastic consumers. No crime victim
incidence studies have yet been published in this
country, but there is no reason to support that what has
been found in Washington and elsewhere does not obtain
here. Nor that further research might not uncover
additional constraints on the reporting of crimes. Thefts

from parents by their own children seem particularly
unlikely to be reported, until they either become so
persistent as to constitute a threat to parental control,
or are used to symbolize an appeal for help with extreme
intra-family conflicts. And small neighbourhood shop-
keepers may hesitate to make official complaints about
petty counter-top thefts of sweets by the children of
neighbours and regular customers.

In Wiltshire and Bristol, victim-instigated inquiries
accounted for more than half the juvenile offence cases
which were processed by the police during the first three
months of 1972. Of the 498 cases in Bristol and the 446
in Wiltshire approximately a third were reported, not by
personal victims, but by the employees of retail and other
types of businesses. The police themselves were directly
responsible for apprehending the next largest group of
children, one in five of the Bristol cases, and one in
ten in Wiltshire.

The nature of the police action which leads to these
notifications is not usually recorded. Some of the
instances followed police responses to the setting off
of alarm bells on industrial or commercial premises.
Others involved the questioning of children 'on suspicion'.
Credit for the remainder presumably must be attributed
either to 'good beat-work' or to the operation of chance
factors. In the second group, the traffic cases, of whom
there were 87 in Bristol and 103 in Wiltshire, chance
plays a far less prominent role, since all but a handful
of them came to notice as a result of straightforward
police activity.

Co-offenders proved a meagre source of suspects; 6 per
cent in both places; surprisingly so in the light of
police claims that most juveniles are easy to interrogate;
guileless once they know the game is up, and eager to co-
operate, by clearing the books of offences to be 'taken
into consideration' for example. Nor were parents,
teachers or social workers any more forthcoming in
reporting children for offence behaviour. In theory, the
1969 Act was designed to do away with the invidious distinctions habitually made between young offenders and
children in need of care. To the people most closely in
touch with children, who must be aware of some of their
many undetected offences, a crime appears still to be a
crime which they are loth to report.

Quite the reverse is the case for the third kind of
child who comes to police notice. These are the so-called
'information' cases and unlike the offenders and the
traffic offenders most of them are not obvious candidates
for court action. They comprise all those children who

are reported to the police or with whom they otherwise
come into contact, and who are not offenders. One
hundred and eighty-four such cases came to the notice of
the Bristol police during the first three months of 1972;
the equivalent figure in Wiltshire was 68. The largest
group amongst them consists of children reported 'missing
from home'. Others are 'found wandering' late at night,
or in 'morally dubious' circumstances; or are discovered
at home without adult supervision. A few are the victims
of parental violence or physical neglect. Parents and
relatives are responsible for drawing the attention of
the police to a much higher proportion of the 'information' cases than is true of crime.

All the offence cases, regardless of who reported
them in the first place, are ones which the constable
involved had decided to take further by making an official
report. There is also one further decision which the
constable has to make. In cases of lesser seriousness
or complexity, e.g., traffic or bye-law offences, he
normally records the details of the relevant behaviour,
takes the name and address of the person involved and
informs him or her that 'the matter will be reported'.
This happened almost invariably in Bristol and Wiltshire
traffic cases. But in more serious cases the officer
has to decide whether to arrest a suspect or not. Not
quite 20 per cent of the Wiltshire children were 'arrested and released', which implies a visit to the nearest
police station. In Bristol nearly 60 per cent were
taken to a police station under arrest, and then released
to parents who had been called to be present during
questioning and the taking of statements. Wiltshire
child-offenders are normally taken home by police
officers and the interrogation and statements conducted
there in the presence of a parent or parents.

From the child's point of view there is probably
little to choose between the felt unpleasantness of the
two methods. And the deterrent effect of going to the
police station may be no greater than being brought home
in a patrol car. But in 'labelling theory' terms being
'taken in' could be construed as more likely to contribute to a deviant self image. If that were so, and it is
a very crude measure, it might be expected that such
children would show up more frequently as subsequent
recidivists. We cannot distinguish, from our data, what
had happened to children in Bristol on previous occasions,
but taken overall, there is not a significantly higher
proportion of recidivists in the study population there
compared with Wiltshire.

The autonomous type of police discretion exercised by

officers on the job, together with the behaviour of
victims and other complainants plays an important part
in defining the kind of offender population which is fed
into the system as the subject matter for the next stage
of the proceedings. This is the formal decision to prosecute or not, which in its turn determines the nature
of the population to be transferred to the courts for the
final part of the process.

Two modes of formal organization can be distinguished,
within which the police in England and Wales make
decisions about juvenile offenders. The first, and the
one employed in Wiltshire, is a 'centralized' model.
Basically this allocates to the constable or investigating officer the task of collecting and collating the
necessary material for a prosecution case which will
stand up in court. Statements have to be taken from
complainants, witnesses and suspects, and a summary
report of the relevant 'facts' submitted without recommendation to an immediate superior, normally the station
sergeant. He checks that the paperwork is in order and
sufficient to prove a case, and then presents it, again
without comment, to his superior; a detective chief
inspector (DCI). The DCI then reviews the evidence in
the file. If he finds it wanting in detail, he may send
it back with a reprimand for poor work and a request for
further information. If the workmanship is satisfactory,
but the substance of a successful prosecution is still
missing, then the file will be marked NFA for No Further
Action and the case closed. When, as in a majority of
cases, the makings of a conviction have been properly
assembled, the DCI considers whether each child merits a
caution or a prosecution. He makes a recommendation on
the file and passes it to his divisional commander,
usually a Chief Superintentent, for final decision and
confirmation. Four ascending levels of the hierarchy
have been involved in this process, which distances the
decision-maker from the events in question. And in
theory, the human or passionate elements of the initial
encounter between the constable and the culprit have been
filtered out by the standard format and dead-pan prose of
the report. Separated in time and organizational space
from the original events, the divisional commander is
enabled to react to each case with a proper disinterest
in the personal implications of his work.

The Wiltshire County police force is organized in
three territorial divisions A, C and D, centred on Salis-
bury, Chippenham and Swindon respectively, so that the
centralized decision-making process is duplicated in each
of them. In addition a Woman Chief Inspector at county

headquarters in Devizes has general responsibility for
liaison with other agencies, principally the social
services departments, and for encouraging the reporting
of 'information' cases by constables.

Juvenile bureaux represent an intermediate or
'specialist' mode of organization for police discretion.
During the 1950s and 1960s a number of forces, more of
them in the north than the south, had set up juvenile
liaison schemes which had extended the procedure of
cautioning into a form of supervision for selected
children.(6)

With the advent of the 1969 Act most, but not all of
these schemes, were wound up, clearly on the premise that
social services departments would be able to handle the
cases thus released. In many places, including Bristol,
the accumulated experience and interest of the juvenile
liaison officers were transferred to the newly formed
juvenile bureaux. Their function is now to vet all the
juvenile cases reported for offences and to decide in
each case whether caution or prosecution is necessary.
Although their decisions are always reviewed, usually by
an inspector in charge of the bureau, and are finally
signed by a chief superintendent, it remains the fact
that discretion is often effectively exercised by individuals of constable rank, as happens in Bristol.

Both the 'centralized' and the 'specialist' organizations for making decisions have two kinds of end product:
a set of decisions; and equally important, a set of
papers. The decisions direct children either onwards
into the judicial system or out of it. The papers,
besides influencing the current decision, also lay the
foundations of a police record which has longer term
implications. One feature of the paperwork which is
particularly pertinent to these decisions is the way in
which specific items of information are selected for
inclusion or omission. In both Wiltshire and Bristol the
papers for offenders are similar. They list basic information about the child followed by a summary of the
incident and, in the case of crimes, are accompanied by
the statements made by the child, by any co-offenders and
by witnesses, including the victim if there is one. This
package of information constitutes a kind of administrative passport which will accompany the child to a decision-
making terminus within the juvenile justice system.

Three main types of data are present in each package:
1. Identifiers – name, age, address, job, school,
                 name of next of kin;
2. Behavioural – the alleged offence or 'charge',
                 place and time of commission, names

                        and ages of co-involved, name and
                        address of victim, value of property
                        involved, value of property
                        recovered;
3. Personal   – family circumstances, home conditions,
                        size of family, position in family,
                        outstanding personal problems or
                        difficulties including physical or
                        mental handicap.

All the identifiers are present in practically 100 per
cent of the cases and they are used initially to conduct
a search for previously recorded contacts between the
juvenile and the police. Previous convictions are confirmed with Criminal Records Office. Previous informal
contacts and cautions are looked up in the Bristol
juvenile bureau's own internal filing system; or they are
sought from the divisional collator's office in Wiltshire.
Behavioural items, with the exception of value of goods,
(22 per cent absent) and complainant (12 per cent absent),
are also present in most of the cases.

Personal data, however, are assembled in a non-
uniform way which has obvious implications for decision-
making. The three items of personal information most
consistently recorded, whether living at home, employment status, and school type, are all inferences from
the 'identifiers' and are not kept in their own right.
No other item is consistently enough present in the police
files of the two areas to suggest that it can have any
significant influence on police decision-making as a
whole. Unrecorded data may of course affect the outcome in individual cases, particularly those where
'consultation' of either a formal or an informal nature
has taken place between the police and any other agency.

Chapter four

Children in trouble : The official picture

Children coming to the notice of the police in Bristol and Wiltshire fall, as we saw in the last chapter, into three groups; offenders, traffic offenders and 'information' cases. For each group we found a distinctive pattern of entry to the status of being known to the police; locally differentiated administrative procedures leading to official decisions, action or inaction; and slightly varying packages of information which were assembled and made available to the decision-makers in these processes. What will be presented in this chapter is in no sense an 'objective' account of the characteristics of these three populations in the two areas. It is rather a description of the information which the police and others have systematically gathered about the children they deal with. It is the 'official picture' of offenders, traffic and 'information' cases. Or more accurately it is a research version of the 'official picture'.

Police records are concerned with two basic descriptive categories; the 'child' and the 'events'; typically offence 'events', in which children become involved. Research studies, including this one, prefer to deal in a different kind of category; the 'population'. This is an artefact produced by the aggregation of individual cases into entities which lend themselves to statistical manipulation; typically the calculation of percentages; the recasting of data into the rows and columns of two, three or more-way tables; and tests of significance.

A sub-variant of the 'population', which we have also employed, is the designation of many individual outcomes, e.g., police or judicial decisions, as an 'output'. Both the 'population' and the 'output' have obvious administrative and research uses. But they are alien both to the working methods of the personnel to whom they are applied,

and to the ways in which they themselves conceptualize
what they do. Even the most casual acquaintance with
people employed in the 'human' services, psychiatrists,
social workers or teachers, reveals what appears to be a
'trained incapacity' to generalize. Their discourse is
predicated on, and their professional ethos is dedicated
to, the unique case. And when they add unique cases
together, the result is not a neat pattern with explicit
surface features, but an essentially unorganized set of
individuals and situations. Their generalizations, if
any are drawn at all, tend towards the anecdotal, the
aphoristic and the allusive, as in: 'Case Z is just like
Case B which I saw years ago.'

As to the validity of the 'facts' on which they base
their judgments and we base our tables, there is no way
of knowing from a study of documentary sources, the true
nature of their relationship to the reality they claim
to depict. But by the practitioners who fashion them and
make use of them in their daily tasks, these 'facts' are
taken as given. They represent, at the moment of their
currency, the authenticated 'administrative truth' about
the situations and actors they speak of. They will be
treated here in the same way, first in relation to
juvenile 'crimes', then to traffic, and finally to
'information' cases.

OFFENCES AND OFFENDERS

The items of information collected by the police can
conveniently be handled under three major heads: the
offence behaviour, the individual offender, and groups
of offenders. Details of behaviour and the individual
child can be drawn directly from the official paperwork
in the form it is first recorded. The characteristics of
groups have to be inferred or extrapolated from the
individual records. It will not be possible to retain
intact throughout this discussion the neat outlines of
such an informational schema, since there is of necessity
a great deal of inter-penetration of data between categories. Separate summaries of the offences and the child
characteristics will therefore be followed by an account
of how they combine in offence-related and group-related
configurations.

Taking the first offence mentioned in the police paper
work, which was typically the most 'serious' in the
official view, the children coming to notice had committed the types of crimes listed in the table below.

TABLE 4.1   Class of first offence by study area
(offenders only)

Offence	Bristol*	Wiltshire
Offences against person	21 (4.3)	27 (6.1)
Offences against property with violence	71 (14.4)	51 (11.4)
Offences against property without violence	304 (61.8)	262 (58.7)
Damage to property	39 (7.9)	61 (13.7)
Forgery, fraud	1 (0.2)	0
Summary offences	33 (6.7)	40 (9.0)
Preventive, trespass	20 (4.1)	2 (0.4)
Traffic**	3 (0.6)	3 (0.7)
Totals	492 (100)	446 (100)

* The Bristol column excludes 6 cases of no information.

**Traffic offences appear in the table in cases where the child has committed a number of offences and the first one recorded is a traffic offence.

Theft is the most prevalent kind of offence behaviour reported, accounting for 60 per cent of the total in both areas. Assaults are few in number, and the teenage vandal is not much in evidence either. If the property theft offences are broken down into a more precise classification then differences emerge between the Bristol and Wiltshire total crime patterns. Shop-lifting offences occur in similar proportions, but there are more burglaries and takings of cars in Bristol, and rather more damage in Wiltshire. Bristol police also arrested a number of children on suspicion alone. Burglary and car-taking may be associated with the built-in opportunities of an urban area, but other factors, to be described later, also affect the Bristol situation.

Two thirds of the offenders commit, or are involved in, only one offence each, although many of them may be members of groups in which larger numbers of offences take place. The victims of their offences are predominantly unrelated adults, just over one third; and business concerns, just under one third. Altogether nearly one half of the offences have personal, as opposed to institutional, victims. And the offences themselves take place

in three typical venues; on the street, on private property, in retail establishments. Where property is
involved, more than half the cases entail cash values of
less than £5. Around 20 per cent involve sums of more
than £16. Schooldays were the most popular days for
committing offences, followed by term-time weekends and
by holidays. Discounting the holidays, which account for
only a small part of our period of study, the most
intriguing fact about time of commission is that in
Bristol, 20 per cent of all juvenile offences were committed during nominal school hours. The presence of
unemployed school leavers in the study population, and
the possible effect of 'grace-and-favour' holidays
granted on unknown dates by individual schools, may
reduce the straightforwardness of this statistic. But
even allowing for all the likely qualifications there
does appear to be a substantial overlap between truancy
and offences.

The official picture of individual offenders and their
personal traits is less detailed and less uniformly
recorded than the one that describes their offence
behaviour. But a number of items is available for all
cases; amongst them the 'identifiers' of sex and age,
plus previous official history. The most obvious division
to be made in our population is between boys and girls
(4:1 in both areas). The sex differential has been pointed
out by many criminologists, but it has rarely been subjected to really close scrutiny, and convincing explanations for it have been proposed even less often.(1) To
the people who actually work in the C & YP system, the
discrepant sex ratio is so commonplace that it seldom
calls forth any comment at all. When the 66 interviewees
in this study were asked to describe the typical case
which they encountered in their work, not one of them
specifically referred to the sex of the offender. A handful alluded to the typical child as 'he' in implicit recog-
nition of the male-female differential. But this absence
of spontaneous mention does not conceal ignorance or
indifference. On the contrary, when specifically asked,
practitioners place the boy-girl ratio at between three
to one and nine to one. Nor were they short of possible
explanations for the phenomenon.

Views were evenly divided between those who ascribed
the differences to the biological and to the social
qualities of both sexes. Boys were seen as aggressive,
adventurous, active, gang-oriented creatures seeking
outlets for their energy and their exhibitionist tenden-
cies through criminal activity. Girls were thought of as
domesticated, solitary, more mature and possibly cleverer

beings, who express their deviance via sexual misconduct
or disturbed behaviour which does not break the law. A
synopsis of these attitudes appears in this reply from a
probation officer:

Men are conventionally more aggressive. The way
society treats the masculine role is to applaud a
certain amount of aggressiveness in men. More scope
for men outside the home. Girls have a feminine role,
caring at home, cleaning and cooking, therefore they
don't go out as much as boys. Aggression is the key
thing. I think the girls will take in inwards the
social deprivation. They will take it by a tendency
towards sexual relationships at an early age, running
away from home. Not an overt, aggressive act which
breaks the law.

Girls in our study population are concentrated in a
much narrower range of offences than boys; shop-lifting
and 'other thefts' account for 90 per cent of them.
'Other thefts' covers a variety of situations, but so far
as shop-lifting is concerned both the boys and the girls
are of similar age spreads and appear to come from
roughly comparable home situations. Their offences are
committed at similar times and involve equivalent values
of merchandise. The nature of the goods taken is,
however, different. Boys tend to go for sweets, comics
or books and instrumental hardware, e.g., records, knives,
torches, radios. Girls take cosmetics, fashion garments
and occasionally accoutrements for their ponies. The
distinction between these sex-specific items is not
simply one of utility versus adornment, since the boys
also steal objects whose primary purpose appears to be
status-inspiring display or consumption.

After sex, age poses another conundrum to the student
of juvenile crime. The annual Criminal Statistics for
England and Wales reveal a peak age for the incidence of
male delinquency which now falls at fourteen years. In
1937 the peak age was thirteen and the post-war shift to
fourteen is sometimes ascribed to the raising of school-
leaving age from fourteen to fifteen which occurred in
April 1947.(2) By this view boys are most susceptible to
delinquency in the year immediately preceding their
departure from school. Why that should be so has yet to
be satisfactorily explained but our data confirm such a
disposition of cases only in Bristol. The Wiltshire boys
appear to reach peak proneness to offences in their
fifteenth year.

In both areas the peak is in any case a relatively
weak one in relation to the numbers for the years which
follow it. Wider data are not available from this study

to indicate whether the discrepancy between the two
areas has anything to do with urban/rural factors, with
police practice, or with differences in educational
systems. But there is some evidence which suggests
differing police approaches to offenders of particular
ages in the two areas.

In Bristol, for example, only 21 children under the
age of ten (4.2 per cent of the total), were dealt with
for offence behaviour. In Wiltshire 61 children of that
age group (13.7 per cent of the total) were picked up by
the police. Being under the age of criminal responsibility, these children can only be screened for possible
care conditions, or returned to their parents by policemen, who may hope that their intervention will have
impressed the child or strengthened the control exercised
in the home. It is possible, but unlikely, that under-
age children in Bristol are three times less likely to
engage in offence behaviour than their contemporaries in
Wiltshire. Or that Bristol victims might be three times
more reticent to report offences involving very young
children.

With the exception of isolated cases which seem somehow to have eluded the filing system, the one item of
personal information most consistently kept by the police
is the record of their previous contacts with particular
children. Past police contacts can take one of three
forms; a previous notification as an 'information', which
can also include children picked up for offences but
adjudicated 'no further action' by the police; a previous
'caution' for an offence; a previous court appearance for
an offence; plus, of course, any combination of these.
Seventy-one per cent of the Bristol children and 85 per
cent of the Wiltshire ones had had no previous court
appearances at all. Less than 10 per cent of them had
been to court on three or more occasions. Superficially
it appears that twice as many of the Bristol offenders
are convicted recidivists than is true of Wiltshire.

Part of the difference is due to the presence in the
Bristol population of a group of highly recidivist
absconders from local remand and community homes. On the
other hand, more children in Wiltshire (20 per cent) than
in Bristol (12 per cent) have previously been cautioned
for the commission of an offence. Whether that reflects
a higher propensity to caution in Wiltshire or a higher
success rate for cautioning in Bristol is something we
shall return to.

It is also possible, from the figures relating to
previous police contacts, to say something about the
assumed overlap between 'care' and 'crime' populations

which lies at the root of much child legislation.
Around 10 per cent of the children currently being processed for committing offences had been previously
recorded as 'information' cases. In the opposite direction 15 per cent of the 'information' cases had previously been to court for criminal matters.

When all three categories of previous notice, caution,
prosecution and information, are combined for the current
offence cases it emerges that about 40 per cent of the
children had had some kind of previous contact with the
police.

CO-OFFENDERS

The Criminal Statistics, annual police returns and the
whole tradition of empirical criminology emphasize and
encourage a view of the juvenile offender as an individual. It is true that explanatory accounts of delinquency,
as they are elaborated from this singular starting point,
do draw in wider social groupings; the family, the school
or the sub-culture, for example. And there is a sizeable
literature on American 'gangs' which tend to be portrayed
as ephemeral phenomena, relevant to only a minor fraction
of delinquent behaviour.(3) Sutherland, in his theory of
'differential association', asserted that criminal behaviour takes place in social situations where the individual's sense of right and wrong is redefined by the
prevailing opinions of more delinquent companions.(4)
But remarkably little is known about the basic micro-
context of most juvenile crime; the small group. This is
hardly ever recognizable as a violent gang situation, but
is most often a small peer group engaging in petty acts
of theft or damage.

In Wiltshire and Bristol only 20 and 21 per cent of
the two offender populations came to police notice for
committing offences by themselves. The children who committed offences with others did so in groups which ranged
in sizes from two to ten. The most typical group is the
pair; but most children take part in events together with
three or more others. These are normally single-sex
groups, but some are mixed-sex groups many of which are
accounted for by the involvement of brothers and sisters
in the same events. One in four of all the groups
actually contained siblings; the larger the membership,
the greater the likelihood that some of them came from
the same family. The age parameters of the groups, the
areas in which the children live, and the schools they
attend, all display a considerable homogeneity amongst

the pairs, which tends to break down as the number of
participants increases. But it is only when a membership
size of five is reached that the age spread, in a majority of groups, begins to exceed two years.

Even a relatively narrow span, however, is sufficient
to bridge the arbitrary age points that mark off the
beginning and the end of the juvenile court jurisdiction.
A few groups in both areas consist only of children under
the age of ten, but almost half the Wiltshire groups and
a third of the Bristol ones contain some children aged
ten to sixteen together with one or more members who are
either below the age of ten or are seventeen and older.
Although the latter are legally classified as 'adults'
most of the over-age offenders are in fact youths of
seventeen or eighteen who are caught in the company of
fifteen- and sixteen-year-olds. Their friendships, whilst
within perfectly natural age limits, just happen to
straddle the line the law has drawn at seventeen. Such
cases present problems to policemen who find themselves
dealing with offenders in two jurisdictions.

The apparently homogeneous basis of delinquent group
membership extends also to the experience of previous
contacts with the police. A majority of the groups include members whose previous records, in the sense of
having one or not, are identical, whilst a sizeable minority consists of children with both types of personal
history. Clearly for those groups in which all the children have a clean sheet, or all have at least one previous
entry in their criminal records, the police decision is
unlikely to pose problems of equity. But in those groups,
approximately one third of the total, where both kinds
are found together, difficulties seem bound to arise.
They will be examined in the next chapter.

GROUPS AND 'SNOWBALLS'

We also distinguished, in our analysis of the basic data,
three types of 'event' configuration:
1. Solo   - single offenders committing one or
                 more offences;
2. Group   - two or more offenders committing one
                 or more offences on the same occasion;
                 and
3. 'Snowball' - two or more offenders committing
                 numbers of offences on diverse
                 occasions.
This did not prove to be as useful a classification as
it had at first promised. Some important differences

were however evident between the members of the three
groupings. Solo offenders in Bristol, for example, are
more frequently represented amongst the under tens and
the sixteen-year-olds, and they show only slight traces
of a peak at fourteen. Nor do Group offenders cluster
significantly at that age, being evenly spread from fourteen to sixteen. It is only the 'Snowball' offenders who
are disproportionately concentrated at age fourteen.

A similar pattern was found to prevail in Wiltshire,
where the peak age across all children occurred at age
fifteen rather than fourteen. Here, Solo and Group offenders are fairly evenly spread from fourteen to sixteen
and, as in Bristol, it is the 'Snowball' boys who pull
the aggregate figure so strongly towards the fifteen-year
mark. If these findings could be replicated elsewhere
they would suggest that the conventional 'delinquency
peak' in the pre-school leaving year is a misleading
'fact', which masks a set of highly differentiated age
distributions by specific offence and by group type as
defined in this study. And that the pre-school leaving
period is not for most children who do offend as delinquency provoking as is sometimes thought.

There is also a small but uniform tendency for Group
offenders to have come to notice less frequently than
either Solo or 'Snowball' children. Solo offenders are
twice as likely to be black as other types; to have
fathers with criminal records, and to have missing
mothers. A higher proportion of 'snowball' offenders
than the other groups were already in the care of the
local authority at the time of committing their current
offence.

The event classification also makes it possible to
test one aspect of the stereotypes concerning boy and
girl offenders which was described earlier. Boys, it was
generally asserted, are social animals, running in packs
which tend to overwhelm whatever private reservations
they might have had about bad behaviour, whereas girls go
singly about their deviant business. In fact the largest
group of girls who do commit offences are shop-lifters.
Compared with boy shop-lifters, the shop-lifting girls in
Bristol are more group prone, not less.

SPECIFIC OFFENCE

Eight classes of offence were specified for this part of
the analysis; assault, burglary, shop-lifting, taking
cars without the owners consent (TWOC), 'other' or
residual thefts, damage, summary, and trespass/suspicion.

The last category applied only to nineteen Bristol cases
about whom little else of interest could be discovered,
except that sixteen of them have no previous court appearances and seventeen have not been previously cautioned.
Arrest on suspicion does not seem therefore to involve
the police 'picking on' known faces for routine 'turn-
overs' or 'liftings' during which, by the law of averages,
some offence behaviour comes to light. Labelling theorists insist that this is one way in which 'deviant
identity' is formed. There is little support for this
notion in these data, and none in what we know about the
children who were first brought to notice as a direct
result of police activity. Hardly any of these, so far
as the records show, were the result of routine stop and
search activities, but the detection by policemen of
children 'in flagrante delicto'.

All the remaining offence categories were compared in
relation to the following attributes: sex, age, number
involved in event, number of offences in event and previous court appearances. Marked differences were
observed between offence types, and between the types in
the two areas, most notably in relation to sex and age.
The concentration of girls in the two offence categories
of 'shop-lifting' and 'other' thefts has already been
noted.

Age provides a particularly rich set of contrasts. In
Wiltshire, for example, assault, TWOC and summary cases
are heavily concentrated amongst the fifteen- and sixteen-
year-olds. In Bristol there is a much wider age spread
in these cases. Damage cases too increase with age in
Wiltshire, but decline in Bristol. And in Wiltshire
relatively substantial numbers of children under ten are
picked up for burglary, shop-lifting and other theft
offences. Assault attracts a higher proportion of solo
offenders than any other offence accounting for a third
of such cases in Bristol, and a half in Wiltshire. In
Bristol solo children are least likely to become involved
in taking cars; and in Wiltshire in committing burglaries.
Shop-lifters tend most often to operate in pairs and
trios. Larger groups, of five or more children, get
caught in the course of burglaries or 'other thefts'.

Gross differences occur too in the number of offences
actually committed during the 'events' of different
offences. Assaults and damage usually comprised a single
occurrence. TWOC offenders accumulated the highest
offence totals for each event, possibly because each car
taken can generate several charges for a single incident.
They were also, by a wide margin, the most recidivist
group of all. More than half of the TWOC boys in both

areas had previously been in court at least once before, and a quarter of them had been two or more times. The least recidivist boys were concentrated in 'other thefts' in Bristol and 'shop-lifting' in Wiltshire. Some of these distributions can be partially accounted for in Bristol by the number of boys already in care who commit TWOC offences.

TRAFFIC

The 'official picture' of traffic offenders is remarkable for its sparsity, and it illustrates a fundamentally different official attitude to traffic offenders. In terms of how much is known about them, there is probably little to distinguish juvenile traffic offenders from adult ones.

Within the juvenile 'traffic' group, failing to display 'L' plates and carrying an unauthorized passenger account for almost two thirds of the total. These are in effect 'status' offences specifically to do with being a learner driver. It would be difficult to construe either offence as representing an immediate physical danger to other road users. And very few instances of careless driving, failing to obey traffic signs, or speeding are reported.

It is significant, perhaps, that 96 per cent of the traffic cases came to notice through the activities of the police themselves and not as the result of complaints by members of the public. And in the absence of specific behavioural offences it must be assumed that youths on scooters and motor-bikes are subjected to systematic checks which uncover the irregularities in question.

With only two exceptions, and as the seating arrangements of motor bikes and scooters imply, the traffic offences are committed either by one person or two. But the limited number of people per offence event is not matched by an equally modest tally of offences since three quarters of the events contain two or more offences. Sixteen-year-olds account for 76 per cent and 83 per cent of traffic offenders in Wiltshire and Bristol respectively; the greater number no longer at school, and working. The proportions of traffic cases with previous court appearances were similar to those of the non-traffic cases; 30 per cent in Bristol, 20 per cent in Wiltshire. Previous cautions too run in parallel, with rather more in Wiltshire (16 per cent) than in Bristol (9 per cent).

The brevity of this portrait of the traffic offender not only accurately reflects police records, but raises a

number of questions about the nature of the whole juvenile jurisdiction and its claim to deal with children 'in
their best interests'; about the way in which the seriousness of offences is assessed, and about police and judicial decision-making. Some of them will be explored in
the next chapter.

'INFORMATIONS'

The most striking thing about the children who are recorded by the police as 'information' cases is that a rough
two to one girl-boy ratio prevails in both areas. This
is the reverse of what was found amongst the offenders.
The overall age distributions of both sexes also distinguish them sharply from the offence cases. Far more
of them fall into the under ten group for instance and in
Bristol as many as a quarter are under the age of six.
In this respect the overlap between the crime and information populations is not so great as the theory of the
juvenile court implies.
     Numbers in Wiltshire are much smaller than in Bristol,
and there are too few boys there to make meaningful any
detailed comparison of the reasons for 'information'
cases coming to police notice in the two areas. The
Wiltshire girls are dominated to an extent not true in
Bristol by the 'moral danger' cases. In Bristol they
come third in order of frequency behind neglected and
missing girls. We have already seen that parents and
other third parties play a much more prominent role in
bringing information cases to police notice than in
offences. There are too few Wiltshire cases to warrant
any sub-division of the 'information' population but the
Bristol boys can be grouped into 'neglect' and a residual
'other' category, and the girls into 'neglect', 'missing
from home' and 'control' cases. Surprisingly perhaps it
is the police who first appear to detect the 'neglect'
conditions in a majority of such cases. We have not
studied the individual cases involved but this may have
something to do with battering cases which are reported
directly to the police by doctors or hospitals. It is
the parents on the other hand who report girls as missing
from home or out of control. The 'neglected' children
are disproportionately drawn from the under five age
group, whilst the missing girls and those who present
control problems are mainly older teenagers.
     The absence of personal data in varying numbers of
cases in both the crime and the information cases makes
any comparison between them as to family structure or

socio-economic status practically impossible. On the
basis of the information we were able to collect there do
not however appear to be any major differences on these
sorts of variables.

THE RAILWAY CHILDREN

There is in this country a number of specially constituted
police forces operating alongside the so-called 'civil'
police. These special forces include the British Transport Police, the British Airports Authority Police, and
the Docks Police. Their officers have all the duties and
powers of police officers within carefully defined limits
and they are, to the casual observer, indistinguishable
in uniform from the civil police. These forces deal, as
one senior officer put it, 'with every crime except
bigamy', and they process a number of juveniles for the
same kinds of incidents as do the civil police. Local
arrangements are made for procedures by which juveniles
may be referred by these forces to the local agencies in a
manner similar to that used by the civil police.
     In the southwest, the main such force in terms of its
area of influence is the British Transport Police, with
an area bordered by Worcester to the north, Bournemouth
to the east, Plymouth to the south, and the river Wye to
the west. Its jurisdiction comprises all property owned
by the British Railways Board, which includes several
main inter-city lines and their attendant stations, and
a number of major goods yards, as well as the engineering
workshops at Swindon. In addition, they have a well-
defined procedure for notifying the local authorities of
any children who may be brought to their notice, and they
bring children to court for offences. Their figures for
the entire region indicated that they were involved with
a significant number of children and it was apparent that
the activities of the British Transport Police, in so far
as they affected juveniles, contributed to the picture of
the handling of juveniles under the Act. This was particularly true of Bristol and Wiltshire, each of which areas
had major British Rail establishments.
     During 1972 the BTP handled a total of 246 cases in
the two study areas, 154 children coming to notice in
Bristol and 92 in Wiltshire. This is a small but not
negligible minority of police work with juveniles, yet it
is a little-known and little-researched area, and it was
therefore decided to devote a special section to the
railway children.
     For two reasons, however, it has not proved possible to

provide full parity of treatment to the BTP as compared
with the main study. The constraints relate first to the
relatively small numbers involved and second to the nature
and quantity of information available. Once the total
BTP population has been broken down into relevant subgroups, the numbers of children become too small, in many
cases, to permit meaningful statistical analysis, and no
attempt was made to apply more sophisticated kinds of
analysis to the BTP data. In addition the 'no information' categories are higher for the BTP children than for
those in the main study. Even 'personal identifiers'
such as age and home address are missing in some instances,
and, while the bare bones of the offence behaviour are
reasonably well documented, many items of personal data
are present on the file in only a minority of cases. In
some ways this is similar to the way in which traffic
cases are handled by the 'civil' police forces and it may
be that many of the BTP offences are similarly seen as
being either trivial or unproblematic.

The children and their behaviour

In contrast to the main study population, an overwhelming
majority of the BTP children fell into the event class of
'offenders'. There were of course, no traffic cases, and
of the 246 children only 13 came into the category of
'care/informations', all of them coming to notice in
Bristol. It will be convenient, therefore, to deal
briefly with the 'informations' before going on to dis-
cuss in more detail the much larger category of offenders.
    These 13 children, 8 boys and 5 girls, were all
checked by BTP for one reason or another at Bristol's
main railway station and found to be missing from home
or from a residential institution. Apart from one ten-
year-old boy, they were in the thirteen to sixteen year
age range, and were all still at school. Nine of the
thirteen were already in care, and two of these were
absconders from custodial institutions. These were not
the only children already in care (absconders or non-
absconders) who came to BTP notice, but the others committed offences and will be dealt with under that heading.
All thirteen children were returned to their respective
homes or institutions and did not become the subject of
further police activity or court proceedings.
    As for the offenders, we find first of all that offen-
ding on railway property is an almost exclusively male
phenomenon. Of 233 offenders in Bristol and Wiltshire,
only 13 (5.6 per cent) were girls, as against 19 per cent

in the main study. They were evenly divided between the
two areas, and the numbers are too small to make worthwhile any separate consideration of the girls. It would
seem that opportunities for the kinds of deviant behaviour
indulged in by girls are not readily available on railway
property.

The age range of children committing offences is shown
in the following table of percentages per age group:

TABLE 4.2   Age range of children committing offences

Age group	Bristol	Wiltshire
< 10 years	11.0%	12.6%
10-12 years	27.8%	31.1%
13-15 years	44.5%	45.9%
16 years	16.8%	10.3%

The two areas are broadly similar, with almost half the
children falling into the thirteen to fifteen age bracket,
but the categories conceal the fact that in Bristol the
peak age is fourteen, while in Wiltshire it is fifteen;
this rather curious variation between areas was also
found in the main study.

There are also differences between the two areas in
terms of recidivism, though not to a significant degree.
Seventy per cent of the Bristol children had no previous
police notice of any kind, but this was true of only 57
per cent of the Wiltshire children, of whom a relatively
high proportion, over one in eight, had three or more
previous experiences of police attention.· The proportions
of children with previous court experiences, however, are
roughly similar. It should be noted that, in contrast to
the main study, there are high proportions of children
about whom no information as to previous official history
was known. This may have something to do with the fact
that the children, particularly in Bristol, were drawn
from a wide area. Only 63 per cent of the Bristol offenders lived in Bristol itself, and over a fifth came from
outside the immediate Bristol area. Almost a tenth of the
Wiltshire children came from outside the county.

Trespassing on railway property is the commonest single
offence in both areas, but whereas in Wiltshire it accounts
for a predominant number of offences (58.7 per cent), in
Bristol there are also large numbers of ticket irregularities and various forms of theft. A small but significant
number of children (10.6 per cent in Bristol and 6.5 per

cent in Wiltshire) were detected in various offences
involving obstruction of the railway line, and in this
group would be included the potentially lethal practice
of stonethrowing. Other forms of vandalism in trains, of
the 'football hooliganism' variety, did not seem to constitute a major threat, in 1972 at least, though perhaps
not all would be reflected in our figures.

It would seem that larger numbers of children were
involved in events in Wiltshire than in Bristol: 15.6 per
cent of the Bristol children were solo offenders, against
6.5 per cent in Wiltshire. Furthermore, of the non-solo
offenders, the majority of the Bristol children took part
in events involving two or three children, whereas 45.7
per cent of all Wiltshire offenders took part in events
involving four children or more. Despite this, however,
the Wiltshire children committed proportionately fewer
offences. Eighty-one and a half per cent of Wiltshire
children committed one offence only and only one child
committed more than two offences, while in Bristol 70.2
per cent committed one offence only and 9.2 per cent committed more than three offences. This apparently paradox-
ical finding, that in Wiltshire larger numbers of children
are involved in smaller numbers of offences, no doubt
reflects the prevalence of trespassing in Wiltshire, and
may be evidence of the Bristol children's greater involvement in ticket frauds and theft being seen as more calcul-
ated or overtly 'criminal' behaviour. In fact, the
trespassers in Bristol seem to be on the whole younger
children and those committing thefts and ticket frauds
older, although the distinction in Wiltshire is less clear
cut.

Finally, a possible way of analysing the BTP offences
is to distinguish between those offences which are
railway-specific (trespassing on the railway line) and
those of the more conventional type. Bearing in mind that
this must be a fairly arbitrary distinction, it is interesting to note that a considerable majority of offences
(69.5 per cent in Bristol and 81.5 per cent in Wiltshire)
were railway-specific. Whether such a distinction is a
significant factor in decision-making will be discussed
later.

The overall picture which emerges is not a particularly
clear one. There is no evidence from our study that the
transport police is dealing with a fundamentally different
population to that of the main police force. Although
there were only one or two instances of the same children
occurring in both the BTP and the main study, there is
evidence of a considerable minority of BTP offenders
having at some time previously come to the notice of the

Bristol and Wiltshire police. Our findings are consistent
with an impressionistic view that the transport police
handle cases of two types: one a relatively large group
of children committing casual, trivial, 'schoolboyish'
offences, of which trespassing is perhaps the best example,
who are dealt with summarily and who are not thought to be
problematic; and second a relatively small group, committing offences against railway property which they may
well have committed elsewhere, perhaps already known to
the police, who are more likely to penetrate further into
the system proper. Such a classification is however tentative and cannot be said to have been established by our
study.

Chapter five

'Without favour or affection':
Police decision-making

Faced with a suspected offender the police can decide to
take one of three courses of action. The offender may be
prosecuted; he may be cautioned; or the case may be marked
'no further action' and closed. 'No further action' or NFA
is viewed by the police as a technical decision which
applies automatically to children under ten who cannot be
prosecuted for an offence, and to older offenders on the
grounds that a case cannot be proved against them in
court. It is not possible, without closer study of the
NFA decisions made in our study population, to say what
proportion of them was prompted by a poor prosecution
case. There were 21 children in Bristol and 61 in Wiltshire who were below the age of ten at the time of their
alleged offences, and who were allocated accordingly to
the NFA category.

But when the two areas are compared as to the use they
made of NFA for offenders aged ten to seventeen, a marked
difference emerges. Bristol police made NFA decisions in
25 per cent of the juvenile offence cases they processed,
more than twice the rate found in Wiltshire where only 10
per cent of the age group was dealt with in this way.
The age distribution of the NFA cases provides one pointer
to an explanation of the disparity. In Wiltshire it is
random; in Bristol it is U-shaped with the under twelves
and the over fifteens being over-represented.

Some of the older children in Bristol belong to a group
of 62 offenders already in the care of local authorities
of whom 20 were eventually adjudicated NFA by the police.
Ten out of 28 in-care Wiltshire children were similarly
decided so that even when these 'in care' cases are
removed, there remains an unexplained difference, which
suggests the possible use of NFA by the Bristol police as
an additional discretionary category. If variations in
the rate of NFA could also be demonstrated elsewhere it

would indicate that conventional caution-prosecution
ratios should be treated with some reserve. More accurate
caution rates might perhaps be expressed as a fraction of
all the relevant offenders known to the police, and not
just of the caution and prosecution totals combined.
Other factors do not seem to relate to the NFA disposition
in a way that makes it possible to speak of a distinctive
profile for such cases; except, that is, for the specific
offence of shop-lifting, which attracts the fewest NFA
decisions in Bristol and the second fewest, after summary
offences, in Wiltshire. This could be due to the relatively cast-iron cases presented by store detectives and
shop-walkers who report many of the thefts in retail
premises. And to the fact that a decision to report the
matter at all may represent a request by a business complainant for positive police action.

The other two police decisions, caution or prosecution,
are superficially more straightforward. In reality they
pose a number of problems to the officers who are responsible for making them. The first of these difficulties
is the absence of a formal legal framework for the practice of cautioning.

Section 5 of the 1969 Children and Young Persons Act
would, if implemented, have provided for the first time
some statutory backing for the police cautioning of juveniles. The decision to suspend Sections 4 and 5 of the Act
means that the only mention in law of cautioning is still
the one in Section 2 of the Street Offences Act 1959,
which allows cautioned prostitutes a right of appeal to
the magistrates court. The Home Office 'Guide' to the
1969 C & YP Act recognizes 'the well established practice
of police forces to caution considerable numbers of juvenile offences'. 'The Act', it affirms, 'does nothing to
inhibit the continuance of this practice...' With this
informal encouragement and the considerable authority of
custom behind them, a number of police forces have devel-
oped criteria for making caution decisions. In the
Metropolitan Police Area these are:

   (a) The offender must admit the offence. In other
       words if the offence is denied an opportunity of a
       court hearing must be allowed to the accused.
   (b) The parents or guardian must agree to the child
       being cautioned.
   (c) The person aggrieved, or loser, must be willing to
       leave the matter in the hands of the police.(1)

Most police forces, including Bristol and Wiltshire,
would probably subscribe to these preconditions even
though they might not formalize them in writing. But
whilst they prescribe the necessary minimum conditions

for a caution they give little positive guidance to an
officer trying to make a decision. London Metropolitan
Juvenile Bureau officers are told that 'suitable cases'
for cautioning would include 'the very young first offender with a stable background'. Otherwise it is suggested
that 'every case is considered on its merits and each
decision based not only on what is considered in the best
interests of the child but also paying due regard to the
interests of the community'. The Bristol and Wiltshire
police forces have made no official statements of cautioning policy, but their practice is affected by another of
the consequences of the 1969 legislation.

'Consultation' is the centre-piece of the informal
arrangements which were substituted for the withdrawn
mandatory provisions of Sections 4 and 5 of the 1969 Act.
Although they lack the force of law, it is unlikely that
any police forces have failed to assemble some sort of
machinery for putting them into effect. In Bristol and
Wiltshire the same basic mechanism is employed. This
takes the form of an automatic written notification to the
local authority for each child coming to police notice.
In Wiltshire the notifications are sent to the social
services department only. In Bristol they go to social
services, education welfare and probation offices as well.
On this, the supply side of consultation, a near 100 per
cent efficiency is achieved. Each child is fully identified and the behaviour which brought him or her to notice
is specified, together with an indication of the likely
police decision in the case. The replies to these forms
from local authorities are of a less predictably efficient
standard and evoke the complaint made by Sir Joseph
Simpson, then Commissioner of Police of the Metropolis, in
his evidence to the Royal Commission on the Penal System
in England and Wales:

> The police and women officers primarily involved in
> dealing with children and young persons feel that
> despite their efforts to help and take an interest in
> the work of local authorities, of children's and prob-
> ation officers, it is a one way operation.(2)

Social services departments, unused to dealing with large
volumes of work in the juvenile courts, found themselves
following 1 January 1971, suddenly inundated with notifications from the police. It had been agreed that to begin
with the probation service was to take responsibility for
all new cases over the age of twelve, but even so the
additional burden on the newly formed social services
departments was considerable. As a result only two types
of cases tend to receive attention from social workers;
those already known to them, usually currently 'live'

cases on an officer's caseload; and unknown cases of
unusual seriousness or persistence.

In Wiltshire during the first three months of 1972, for
example, the social services department reported to the
police that they knew or had made inquiries about 39
offenders out of the 446 of which they were notified.   In
the majority of the remaining cases the police were informed that the child was 'not known' to the department.
Interviews with senior police officers, and with team
leaders in each of the Wiltshire social services areas,
disclosed a situation in which scarcely any discussion of
individual offenders took place beyond this exchange of
papers.   Some individual cases in which consultation had
occurred were mentioned by name.   In many places, no
formal consultation cases could be recalled during the
twelve months preceding the interview.   Some informal
contacts may well have taken place, both personally and
by telephone, but they were nowhere recorded in the police
paperwork.

Wiltshire social workers did not seem too down-hearted
about their apparent inability to make a more substantial
contribution to the police decision-making process.   Some
were fatalistic about their chances of ever changing what
they saw as the firm decisions already made by the police.
Others however were keen to see many more inquiries made
into the personal circumstances of offenders when
resources of staff time and general priorities permitted.

In Bristol the existence of a juvenile bureau manned
by specialist officers created a different situation but
one with uncertain results.   Bureau officers often took
the initiative in seeking information from other agencies,
particularly where there was evidence of their prior
involvement with an individual child.   A lot of this
informal consultation took place over the telephone or in
personal contacts which were not necessarily recorded in
the police files.   Otherwise we could trace only 54
written replies from Bristol social services department;
not all of them relating to offenders; and 50 of them
reporting that the child was 'not known'.   Since 792
children who had offended, committed traffic offences, or
come to notice as 'information' cases, were known to the
Bristol police during this period, it suggests that a
fully reciprocal form of consultation was still, at that
time, undeveloped.   A research strategy based on documentary sources, as ours was, can therefore throw little
light on the nature and effectiveness of social work
intervention in Bristol police decisions.

Our methodology has also precluded any consideration
of some of the issues arising from previous studies of

police discretion. An interactionist perspective has for
example led Skolnick; Piliavin and Briar; Emerson;
Cicourel and others to stress the situational aspects of
police and judicial decision-making.(3) They have focused on the occupational cultures of the patrolman and
the social worker which affect their attempts to establish
the moral character of the suspects they encounter. And
Wilson has elaborated a typology of police organization
'styles' each of which, he claims, is accompanied by a
distinctive pattern of arrest and disposition.(4)

But two other research traditions are of direct relev-
ance to this study. The first of them examines individual
differences in decision-makers. Work by Green; Wilkins
and Chandler; Gottfredson; Hood; Hogarth; and Wheeler has
sought to relate personal characteristics such as age,
sex, length of service, and in some cases attitudinal
data, to the real or simulated decision-making outputs of
their subjects.(5) Some of our findings in this area
will be presented later in this chapter. The second set
of relevant research studies isolates single factors or
clusters of factors which appear to discriminate between
individuals with different destinations in the decision-
making system; see for example studies by Grünhut;
Goldman; McEachern and Taylor; Wolfgang, Figlio and
Sellin; Avison and McClintock; Hohenstein; and Terry.(6)

Since most of this work has been done in the USA much
of it is concerned with the effect of race on police or
court decisions. Although there are contradictory findings, many of them report that black juveniles are more
likely to be arrested, prosecuted and kept in custody
than are white children, even when other possibly influ-
ential factors are held constant. Only forty children
from ethnic minorities could be identified in the offender
populations we assembled in Bristol and Wiltshire, which
is too few to make the question meaningful in our analysis.

Apart from race, however, many of these studies agree
that police decisions are influenced by the age and sex
of the offender, by the 'seriousness' of the offence committed, and by his or her previous history of contacts
with the police or the courts.

AGE

The Criminal Statistics for England and Wales have recorded annual rates of cautioning since 1954. They deal only
in raw totals and are flawed by the omission of 'no
further action' decisions; but they do portray an unmistak-
able growth in the practice. One way of illustrating its

impact on juveniles is to observe the age at which the
proportion of boys or girls cautioned for indictable
offences moves above the 50 per cent mark. Between 1962
and the end of 1970, girls aged ten, eleven, twelve and
thirteen had passed this mark, as had boys aged ten and
eleven. In 1971 following the implementation of the 1969
Act there was a visible surge in the trend. In that year
girls aged fourteen, fifteen and sixteen and boys aged
twelve and thirteen all became more liable to caution than
to prosecution. Fourteen-year-old boys are currently
approaching a position of parity between the two dispositions, but fifteen- and sixteen-year-old boys are still
much more likely to be prosecuted than cautioned.

Because they contain 'no further action' cases, the
decisions made by the police in Bristol and Wiltshire are
not strictly comparable with the national figures. But
they reflect a broadly similar picture in which boys and
older children are more likely to be prosecuted than girls
and younger children respectively. Goldman's study of
police discretion in four American 'municipalities' shows
a court referral rate of around 30 per cent for each age
group between nine and thirteen. From age fourteen onwards the rate increased steeply to just under 50 per
cent for the seventeen-year-olds.

Our data for boy offenders, aged ten to seventeen only,
reveal a distinctive three-part structuring of prosecution
rates by age, which is shown in figure 1, and in both
Wiltshire and Bristol there appears to be a group of
young boys who are (a) less likely to come to police
notice at all, and (b) if they do, are far less likely
than their older peers to be prosecuted. An intermediate
age range forms a plateau in both graphs during which a
prosecution rate of between 33 and 40 per cent prevails.
These plateaux do not however coincide in the two places;
the Bristol one begins at age thirteen and finishes at
fifteen; one year later than in Wiltshire where it runs
from twelve to fourteen. The third level comprises the
fifteen- and sixteen-year-old boys in Wiltshire, and the
sixteen-year-olds in Bristol. Both these groups are
subject to much higher prosecution rates than the
younger ones; about two thirds and one half respectively.
Too few girls came to notice for the commission of
offences to make possible an equally reliable breakdown
of their prosecution rates by age, but a broadly comparable pattern does seem to apply to them as well. All our
efforts to account for this plateau configuration in
terms of other factors such as the type or seriousness of
offences committed by boys of different ages, or the
longer police records of older youths, failed to destroy

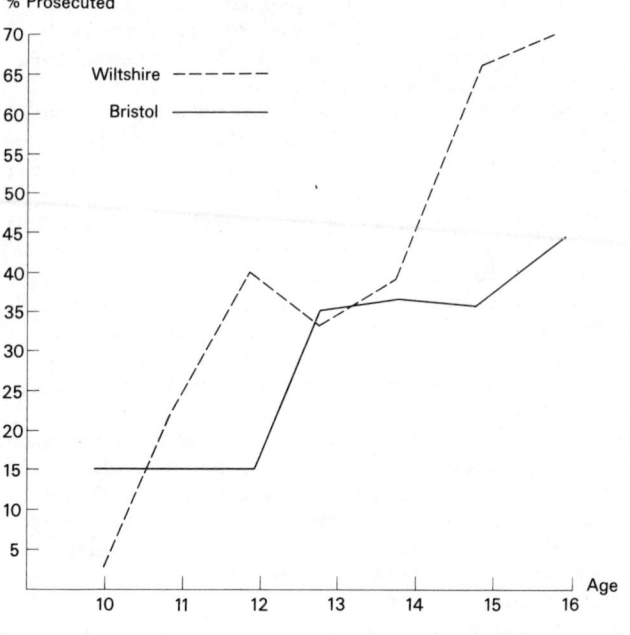

FIGURE 1   Children prosecuted in Wiltshire and Bristol

the original finding. A smoothly progressive curve of
increasing prosecution by age would have required little
explanation, but a stepped structure of the kind described
here invites some kind of interpretation and this will be
attempted in the final chapter. It is not possible to
check the finding against national figures which are for
indictable offences only, and do not include 'no further
action' decisions.

'SERIOUSNESS'

The idea of a tariff dominates everyday thinking about
the determination of court sentences. More serious
offences are thought to merit heavier penalties, and
repeated re-appearances before a court, even for the same
trivial kind of behaviour, are often held to justify the
eventual imposition of a disproportionately 'severe'
sentence. It may be that police decisions are made in
the same way. In this section the notion of 'seriousness'
and its possible impact on police discretion will be

explored. The effect of an offender's previous record
will be looked at later.

The 'seriousness' of an offence is an obviously subjective judgment but there are a number of ways in which a
more public meaning of the term can be arrived at. In
English law there is a rudimentary division of all
offences into 'indictable' or more serious crimes, and
'non-indictable' or less serious ones. Another order of
gravity is implied by the maximum sentences which offences
attract. And a common-sense ranking can be construed from
the Home Office classification used for annual police
returns of criminal statistics. This works its way down
from murder at the top, through a variety of assaults to
ordinary larcenies, and it terminates in the least serious
summary offences and breaches of administrative law. The
defects of the scheme stem from the infidelity of human
behaviour to the categories thus established. Burglaries
for instance may be legally classified as more serious
than simple larcenies, but the size or sentimental value
of the goods involved, or the personal reactions of the
victims, can greatly reduce the validity of the rating.

An alternative approach is to ask relevant actors in
the criminal justice system to assign levels of seriousness to specific types of offences.(7) This was done in
the present study in two ways; first by asking the 66
practitioners who we interviewed to nominate 'most serious'
and 'most trivial' offences. Fifty of them thought that
violence was the 'most serious' kind of behaviour. Vandalism and breaking-in came second and third, but a long
way behind violence. The 'most trivial' offences, in
descending order of triviality, were thought to be
traffic, riding a bicycle without lights and petty theft
or shop-lifting.

Second, the practitioners were asked to rate the four
'most serious', and the four 'least serious' from the
following random order list of offences:

exceeding the speed limit	theft from parents
obstructing railway line	air rifle uncovered
assault occasioning actual	taking a vehicle without the
bodily harm	owner's consent
burglary	theft of 50p from a house
breach of the peace	carrying an unauthorized
no insurance on a motor	passenger
cycle	theft from a shop
arson	criminal damage, value £5
indecent assault	theft of £10 from a house

The offences are not an exhaustive list, but were intended to represent a normal spectrum of cases likely to be
encountered in the administration of juvenile justice.

Sixty-two usable ratings were obtained in which the listed
offences appeared to fall into three groups of approximately equal size. The 'most serious' group comprised
assault occasioning actual bodily harm, arson, obstructing
the railway line, indecent assault and burglary.

An intermediate group of little mentioned offences were
seen as neither serious nor trivial, e.g., damage, theft
of 50p, no insurance, TWOC, shop-lifting and theft of £10.
And the 'least serious' group consisted of theft from
parents, breach of the peace, speeding, uncovered air
rifle and carrying an unauthorized passenger. The three
groups, from 'most' to 'least serious', can be broadly
characterized as 'offences against the person', 'offences
against property' and 'breaches of regulations'. It is a
conventional and not unexpected evaluation of offence
seriousness, but as a predictor of how such cases are
dealt with in practice it proves to be somewhat deficient.
If a police decision to prosecute is taken to recognize,
amongst other things, the seriousness of an offender's
behaviour, and if the rankings we have obtained from these
two exercises are accepted as accurate reflections of
professional opinion on this matter, then we might expect
to find that violent offenders and burglars are amongst
the most likely candidates for prosecution. What we find
in fact is rather different.

TABLE 5.1   Rates of prosecution by offence

Offence	Bristol	Offence	Wiltshire
TWOC	50.0%	TWOC	82.3%
Summary	44.0%	Summary	67.2%
Burglary	40.3%	Assaults	66.6%
Other thefts	33.3%	Other thefts	45.9%
Damage	22.8%	Damage	43.6%
Shop-lifting	21.2%	Burglary	39.4%
Assaults	16.6%	Shop-lifting	20.3%

In Bristol the assault cases are the least likely to
be prosecuted, and in Wiltshire children who commit burglaries are the second least likely to end up in court.
The practitioners do achieve one modest predictive success
in that theft from shops is not only low in their evaluation of seriousness but also attracts a low rate of prosecution in practice. Taking cars without the owners

consent is the most often prosecuted offence in both
areas, a finding which confirms what Goldman and McEachern
have separately reported about the self-evident seriousness of car theft in policemen's eyes.(8)

The apparent reversal of common sense in these results
can be resolved to some extent by looking again at the
ages of the boys who are caught committing various types
of offence. Assaults and damage are disproportionately
the work of younger boys; whilst taking cars and summary
offences seem to appeal more to older ones. A breakdown
of prosecution rates by specific offence also permits a
fresh look at the apparent sex-discrimination in police
decisions. Both the national Criminal Statistics and the
findings of this research indicate that girls appear to
enjoy a lower rate of prosecution than the boys. Girl
offenders can be divided into two groups; those who steal
from shops, and those who engage in miscellaneous larcenies elsewhere. In Wiltshire, too few girls are prosecuted
to make possible a proper comparison, but in Bristol there
were as many girls as boys who came to notice for shop-
lifting. Exactly the same proportion of both sexes was
prosecuted by the police, which suggests that girls do not
receive favourably differential treatment when offence is
controlled for.

There are three further but cruder measures of seriousness to be derived from our material; the policeman's
decision to arrest, the number of offences committed by
each child, and the value of goods involved in property
offences. All three proved to be positively related to an
eventual decision to prosecute. Thus, being arrested by a
policeman, committing more than one offence, and stealing
goods worth more than £5 are factors which forecast more
accurately the fate of an individual offender than do the
private estimates of offence seriousness made by policemen, social workers and magistrates.

TRAFFIC

There is, however, one aspect of these ratings which
deserves closer attention. It concerns the low seriousness status of traffic offences in the responses of the
interviewees, which contrasts sharply with what happens
in practice to the boys who are apprehended for committing
them. In Bristol the traffic offenders were more likely
to be prosecuted than those in any other category, including TWOC. This may be due to the fact that at the time
of this study juvenile traffic cases were being dealt with
in Bristol by policemen working in divisional process

offices and not by the juvenile bureau. It may also have
something to do with the route by which most traffic cases
come to notice, and the nature of the offences with which
they are charged. Almost all traffic offenders are
caught by police activity and are hardly ever reported by
members of the public or by individuals who are in any
sense aggrieved by their behaviour. And most of their
offences are status based, such as having no 'L' plates
or carrying an unauthorized passenger. These are offences
for which no criminal intent need be proved and to which
there is no adequate legal defence.

In Wiltshire, the prosecution rate for traffic offenders is the fourth highest, after car-taking, summary
offences and assaults. It could be argued that these
traffic cases are prosecuted more often simply because
most of the boys who commit them are fifteen- or sixteen-
year-olds. If the prosecution rates for sixteen-year-old
traffic and non-traffic offenders are compared, however,
the traffic cases, particularly in Bristol, are still more
liable to prosecution. And if the traffic offences themselves are specified in more detail, a subsidiary hierarchy of prosecution rates emerges there as well. One
hundred per cent of the no-insurance cases are taken to
court. 'L' plate and passenger offences form an intermediate group and all the other traffic cases taken
together are the least liable to prosecution.

The treatment of juvenile traffic cases raises interesting questions which will be pursued in the next two
chapters. At this point in the discussion it is worth
noting that juvenile traffic offenders appear to be
excluded from the arrangements for consultation between
police and social work agencies. The practitioners who
were interviewed had not only voted traffic cases into
the least serious category of offences; they also took
the view that the juveniles who committed them were not
in need of help in the way that non-traffic offenders
often were.

PREVIOUS RECORD

If the police decision to prosecute children were found
to conform to some kind of tariff system, the two most
obvious factors on which it might rest are the seriousness of the offence committed and the previous record of
the individual offender. Seriousness, as we have seen, is
not a simple matter and our ex-post-facto findings did not
agree too well with the predictions we had derived from
the views of the people working in the system. So far as

previous police contacts are concerned a tariff suggests
two things. First, that previously cautioned children
would be much more liable to prosecution on the second
occasion they came to police notice and, second, that
previously prosecuted children would be unlikely to receive
cautions for any subsequent offence they committed.

Past contacts with the police can take one of three
forms: convictions, cautions, or 'informations' which also
include some decisions to take 'no further action' in
respect of an alleged offence. Around 40 per cent of the
offenders in the Bristol and Wiltshire study populations
had a previous record of some sort. Between 20 and 30 per
cent had appeared in court; 12 to 20 per cent had been
cautioned and approximately 10 per cent were recorded as
previous information cases.

In Bristol, children who had prior informations were
less likely to be cautioned when they reappeared than were
those with none. And of 53 Bristol children already
cautioned for past offences, only 20 were prosecuted, a
proportion not markedly different from the one for children with no previous cautions. In Wiltshire all three
classes of previous notice on a child's record proved to
be positively associated with a police decision to prosecute. Although the possible overlap between one kind of
previous notice and another makes these figures rather
difficult to interpret, the Bristol ones do not support
the idea of a police tariff by which previously cautioned
children are automatically prosecuted if they offend
again. Possession of a court record however, doubles the
rate of prosecution over the one that obtains for the
non-recidivists. The effect in Wiltshire is to raise the
prosecution rate for boys from 35 to over 70 per cent.
But in Bristol just over half of the recidivists continue
to escape prosecution. Previous convictions also reduce
the chances of a traffic offender avoiding prosecution.

WELFARE-RELATED ITEMS

Items like sex, age, specific offence and previous record
were all available in police files in practically 100 per
cent of the cases. Other descriptive details about the
home backgrounds of children were less systematically
assembled, and presumably less often referred to in the
decision-making process. Statistics which refer to only
60 or even 80 per cent of a population need to be treated
cautiously but they can act as pointers to areas of interest. There is for example a widely held theory in 'lay'
criminology that working mothers are a prime cause of

crime amongst their 'latch key' children. Of the children
with working mothers known to the police in Bristol and
Wiltshire a significantly higher proportion were prosecuted compared with those whose mothers did not go out to
work. But this apparent confirmation of everyday theory
can also be interpreted in a different way. It is
possible that police officers who are aware of the stereo-
type make special efforts to find out, in cases where
they may already be considering a prosecution, whether
this factor is present in the family of the offender or
not.

Other family factors found to be significantly related
to the decision to prosecute included the presence of
substitute fathers or mothers, i.e., 'broken' families;
fathers or mothers with criminal records; and low socio-
economic status. Belonging to a family with five or
more children in it, or occupying an intermediate birth
order position appeared relevant in Wiltshire only.
Bristol children who lived on council estates were more
likely to be prosecuted than their peers who lived elsewhere. Without further data and additional analysis not
much reliance can be placed on these results, but there
is one final finding of a minor nature to be reported.
Since it concerns the initial letters of children's
surnames, it is not qualified by a large 'no information'
category.

The effect of alphabetic name order on school achieve-
ment has been examined in a number of studies, but with
inconclusive results. Weston, on the other hand, has
reported that hospital referrals for stomach ulcers and
for neurosis were disproportionately drawn from individuals whose surnames began with letters S to Z.(9) When
the surname initials of juvenile offenders in the present
study were dichotomized A to E and F to Z, and set
against the police decision to caution or prosecute,
children in the first group were found to attract a
lower rate of prosecutions than those whose names came
later in the alphabet. This result is significant at the
5 per cent level in Wiltshire and although it falls just
short of significance in Bristol it is skewed in the same
direction. Work on children's christian names suggests
that those with uncommon ones are held in lower esteem by
their peers.(10) Our finding on surnames is not a particularly strong one but it might indicate that some kind
of unstated status attaches to names at the beginning of
the alphabet.

POLICE DECISION-MAKERS

Considerable evidence exists that individual decision-makers can reach quite divergent conclusions from the same information. It would be surprising if the same effect were not to be found in the working of the Children and Young Persons Act 1969. In Wiltshire the decisions can not be so clearly ascribed to individual policemen as in Bristol, since the divisional chief inspector is not always the same person. There are signs of inter-divisional differences in the Wiltshire police decisions, but because deputies for the DCI are frequently involved in their making, we have not pursued them further.

In Bristol the decision-making output of the Juvenile Bureau officers was readily accessible in our data. They reveal individual prosecution rates for boys which range from 24 to 47 per cent. The numbers of cases decided by each officer were too small to permit even two-way tables to be constructed with confidence. Officers were combined therefore into a high-prosecution group and a low-prosecution group, and some of the key characteristics of their cases examined. Age and specific offence did not appear to be differentially distributed between the cases decided by the two groups. Boys with previous court records were disproportionately concentrated in one group's cases; but contrary to expectations it was the 'low' rather than the 'high' prosecution rate group. It may be that factors not controlled for here, e.g., the value of goods stolen, or the presence of 'in-care' cases, are responsible for the differences in prosecution rates. But the analysis, so far as it goes, suggests the possibility of a personal factor at work in the decision-making of juvenile bureau officers. Support for this conclusion was also provided by the results of a small-scale decision-making exercise administered to all bureau officers in Bristol and to five senior officers in Wiltshire. In 6 out of the 11 hypothetical cases they were asked to consider, the officers achieved unanimity or near unanimity in their decisions to caution or prosecute. In the remaining 5 cases there were substantial differences of opinion which split the officers in varying proportions between the two decisions.

PREDICTIVE ATTRIBUTE ANALYSIS

So far in this chapter a number of factors both singly and in combination have been related to police decisions

to caution or to prosecute. But simply listing some positive correlations, together with some subsidiary findings
obtained by holding other factors constant, leaves un-
explored the question of relationships between independent
variables. Factor analysis is designed to perform this
kind of function but was, for technical reasons, inappropriate to our data. It was decided therefore to employ
Predictive Attribute Analysis (PAA), a technique devel-
oped by Wilkins and McNaughton-Smith (11) which yields
not only a set of correlates with a pre-determined variable (in this case, police decision), but places the
crucial factors in a hierarchical, branching structure:
figures 2 and 3. The original population is divided into
two subgroups according to the presence or absence of an
attribute which is found to be most closely associated,
as measured by X^2, with the pre-determined variable.
This attribute having been eliminated, the two resulting
groups are then further divided by the same process,
giving four subgroups of the original population. This
procedure, which is referred to as 'splitting', is repeated
until the subgroups produced either become too small for
statistical purposes, or no clear association with the
pre-determined variable is apparent within them. The end
product of the sequence of splits is a set of subgroups,
internally homogeneous, but highly differentiated from
each other.

The method requires a simple two-state criterion which
entailed a choice between the following possible ways of
dividing police decisions:
   (a) 'no further action' plus caution/prosecution
   (b) 'no further action'/caution plus prosecution
   (c) caution/prosecution.
On the assumption that 'no further action' is a decision
which precedes any consideration of caution or prosecution it was decided to exclude it from the analysis.
This has the advantage of revealing the net characteristics of the cautioned and prosecuted groups, but it
also forfeits the chance to learn something about the
differential use of 'no further action' by the police
forces in the two areas. A separate PAA exercise based
on the split between 'no further action' and the two
other decisions would be necessary for this purpose.
Forty items were selected for testing against the police
decision to prosecute. All of them were dichotomized,
some only once, as in 'male-female', others, such as age,
in several ways so as to exhaust the possibilities of the
category. This produced a total of ninety-four dichot-
omies.

The results of the PAA for Bristol and Wiltshire are

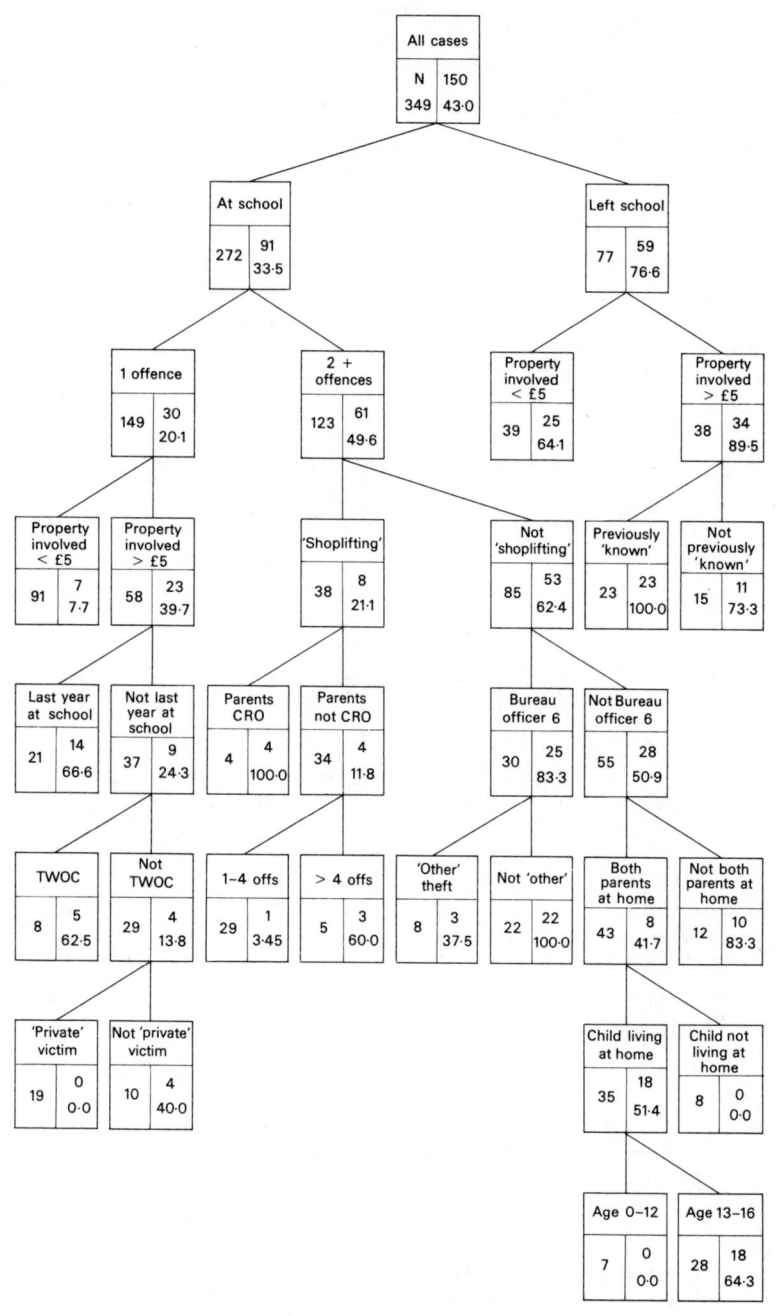

FIGURE 2 Predictive attribute analysis - Bristol

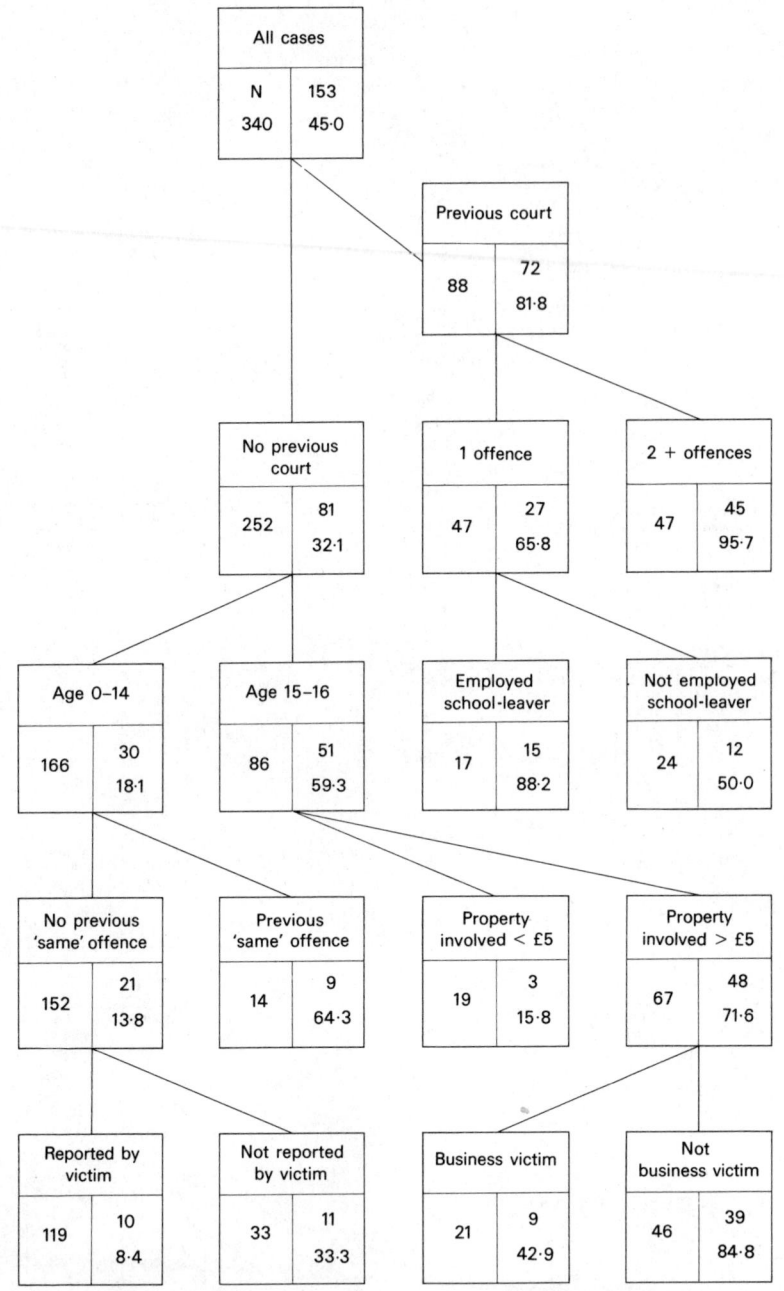

FIGURE 3 Predictive attribute analysis - Wiltshire

set out in figures 2 and 3. The most salient feature of
the two presentations is the more elaborated nature of
the Bristol 'tree' compared with the Wiltshire one. But
closer inspection of the splitting factors does not
reveal any radical differences between the two areas. In
Bristol the first split occurs on the age-related factor
of 'at school/left school'; the school-leavers being the
more likely to be prosecuted. In Wiltshire the first
split relates to the possession of a previous court
appearance. If the subsequent factors in the first four
sets of splits are compared, the same restricted range is
found in both; age, previous convictions, school status,
number and value of offences. Although these factors
occur in different configurations in the two 'trees', they
do confirm our earlier findings that police decisions as
a whole are not based on 'welfare' related items in the
personal backgrounds of the children they deal with. They
are apparently much more influenced by the 'seriousness'
of their offence behaviour, as measured by relatively
simple criteria, and by the age and previous criminal
history of the offenders. Sex, interestingly, never came
close to splitting any of the groups in the PAA. The
fact that the first Bristol split was on school-leavers
lends additional weight to the 'plateau' effect of increasing age on prosecution rates discussed earlier, and,
whilst school-leaver status refers predominantly to
sixteen-year-olds in Bristol, the group of Wiltshire
children with no previous court appearances is next
split at age fourteen, which isolates as a higher prosecution risk the fifteen- and sixteen-year-olds, both
results running in parallel to the 'plateau' effect.

The PAA also isolates subgroups in the total offender
populations with very high and very low prosecution rates.
In Wiltshire for example 95 per cent of children with
previous court appearances who commit more than two
offences are prosecuted, as are 85 per cent of those with
no previous court appearances but who are aged fifteen or
sixteen and steal goods worth more than £5 from a non-
business victim. The Wiltshire children least likely to
be prosecuted were those with no previous court appearances, aged under fourteen, with no prior notification
for an offence of the same class and who were reported by
their victims rather than anybody else. In Bristol 100
per cent of the school-leavers who stole goods worth more
than £5 and who had some kind of previous record were
prosecuted. At the other extreme Bristol school-children
who committed one offence involving goods worth less than
£5, who were not within three terms of leaving school, had
not taken a car without the owner's consent, and whose

victims were private individuals were all cautioned.

Later splits in the Bristol PAA are caused by factors
which do not figure at all in the Wiltshire one.   A
juvenile bureau officer for instance appears as a splitting variable, as does the parental structure of the
offenders' families. It might be thought that the presence of such an item in the Bristol PAA indicates a more
child-oriented approach on the part of the police there.
But the appearance of a juvenile bureau officer suggests
that it may simply reflect the personal concerns of one of
a number of decision-makers. Overall the analysis reveals
a situation in which the decision to prosecute is taken by
the two police departments mainly on the basis of a few
simple factors, which with the exception of age, appear to
exclude any which would normally be thought of as relevant
to the 'interests of the child'. Public protection and
the punishment of older and more serious offenders seems
to inform a majority of the police decisions we studied.

One final aspect of police discretion remains to be
considered. Children who commit offences do not do so
only as individuals; many of them operate in groups. What
impact, if any, does this fact have on the decisions made
by the police?

CO-OFFENDERS

Faced with a group of suspected offenders the police can
decide to take one of three courses of action. Excluding
the 'no further action' option, all the offenders may be
cautioned, all the offenders may be prosecuted, or the
members of the group may be split between the two dispositions in some way. Four fifths of the offenders in this
study committed their misdeeds in the company of other
children, which makes group membership and its effect on
police decisions a particularly crucial one.

Two thirds of the practitioners we interviewed agreed
that juvenile delinquent groups typically comprised the
leaders and the led. Two types of leader were distinguished in their replies; a conventional one who is the
child with a stronger personality; and a lesser known
'leader from behind', who instigates or manipulates other
children into actually committing an offence whilst he
keeps out of the way and avoids the legal consequences.
But what appeared to some to be leadership, was seen by
others as a group phenomenon: 'Group activity can often be
stimulated by group discussion, conversation and opinion
until a situation is reached when nobody can duck out of
what takes place', said one policeman. This general

agreement about group structure did not however survive
when the question of its effect on the idea of personal
responsibility for behaviour was raised. Rather more than
a third of the policemen, social workers and magistrates
asserted that easily led children could not be held fully
responsible for what they did.

An equally sized group took the opposite view: 'In the
eyes of the law they are still responsible for their
actions. It is a weakness of character isn't it? They
have to be taught the difference between right and wrong
to prevent further trouble', was how a social worker
expressed it. And the same split views spilled over into
the solutions proposed by the practitioners to a basic
decision-making dilemma; namely, should all the members
of a delinquent group be dealt with in the same way or
differently? It is a question which goes to the heart of
the justice-versus-welfare tension referred to in chapter
2. Two kinds of answers to it can be presented here;
what the practitioners say they do; and what they actually
appear to do. Only a minority of the interviewees was
unequivocally in favour of equal treatment for all the
members of a delinquent group. A majority, including
many policemen, supported the idea of individualized and
discretionary treatment measures for each of the members
of a group. Such a response is consistent with the
'spirit of the Act' but what happens in practice runs
counter to these professions of therapeutic intent.

In Bristol, 123 delinquent groups fell within the time
parameters of this study; in Wiltshire there were 122.
Police decisions which actually split the members of
these groups between caution and prosecution outcomes
were made in only four of the Bristol events, and in nine
of the Wiltshire ones. There is little to be said stat-
istically about so few instances, and not much more that
can be added impressionistically.

For the groups which were split in this way, four
seemed to be a typical membership; of whom two were
cautioned and two prosecuted. The cautioned members
seemed to be those who took the least active parts in
'snowball' type events. They were not necessarily the
ones with the fewest previous convictions.

But making different decisions about offenders who
have all been caught doing the same thing is not the only
way in which police discretion affects the members of
delinquent groups. There are also situations in which
they make the same decisions about children who have
different criminal histories. Within the groups where
all the participants were given the same police decision,
there were three patterns of previous police records;

those in which:
   (a) all the members have no previous record of any
       sort;
   (b) all the members do have a previous record; and
   (c) there is a mixture of first-timers and recidivists.
   When all the members of a group are being apprehended
for the first time they are most likely to be cautioned.
When all the members have a previous record, they are more
likely to be prosecuted. But when the membership of a
group is a mixture of first offenders and recidivists the
chances of caution and prosecution are about even.
Clearly these mixed membership groups face the police in
both areas with a finely balanced calculus of interests.
Should they prosecute all the members regardless of record
in order to bring to court one or two recidivists who have
already been cautioned or prosecuted? Or should they
split the group in order to protect the less criminally
experienced members from a court appearance? Or should
they actually caution one or two 'bad lots' who appear to
have led on other children whose antecedents do not merit
prosecution at this stage? We have seen that the splitting
of groups occurs only infrequently. The police appear to
resolve the dilemma by assessing such mixed groups corpor-
ately in terms of the number and distribution of their own
previous contacts with its members. This is evident from
the lower average number of previous contacts for the
members of those mixed groups who are all cautioned rather
than all prosecuted. There is one further way in which
group membership may affect police decision-making. It
concerns those juveniles who are reported for committing
offences with 'adults'. There were 50 such events in
Wiltshire and 25 in Bristol. In three quarters of these
events all the members, both adult and juvenile, were
prosecuted. Many of the juveniles in these events were
boys of sixteen and the way they were dealt with may
partly account for the high rate of prosecution which
characterizes this age group.

BRITISH TRANSPORT POLICE DECISIONS

The decision-making process in the British Transport
Police differs from that described for the Bristol and
Wiltshire police in that the options for railway policemen include what might be described as an informal
caution, administered to an offender on the spot without
further enquiries, and recorded as an 'unofficial'
caution. It is therefore difficult to compare cautioning
figures with those found in the main study, since the

criteria are not likely to be the same, and, moreover, children below the age of responsibility, who would in the main study have been automatically classed as 'no further action' cases are recorded as having been cautioned. Since total numbers at risk of receiving a caution are therefore higher than total numbers at risk of being prosecuted, care should be taken in drawing conclusions from a direct comparison, and such comparisons as will be made in this section between the BTP and the civil police are tentative.

Although a really thoroughgoing study of BTP discretion is not feasible owing to the small numbers of cases in certain categories and the limited amount of information available on many items, it is possible to identify a number of factors which lead to a relatively high risk of prosecution. Overall, the BTP prosecuted fewer children and cautioned more than either the Bristol or Wiltshire forces.

The factors which lead to a prosecution can be discussed under two main headings: personal and behavioural.

As in the main study, older children were more likely to be taken to court: almost half the sixteen-year-olds were prosecuted. Below that age, however, the picture is far from clear; for Wiltshire children there is a smoothly rising graph of prosecution rates, but for the Bristol group no clear pattern emerges. The same finding is reflected in the employment status of the child. Being still at school after the then statutory leaving age of fifteen did not confer the same degree of protection as it did in the main study, but children who had left school were still prosecuted in greater numbers than children who had not, particularly in Wiltshire. In marked contrast to the findings of the main study the child's previous record did not seem to exert any great influence on his fate. Children from Bristol with no previous notice were prosecuted at about the same rate as those with, and in Wiltshire a third of those with no previous notice were prosecuted as against one quarter overall. The situation is complicated by the number of cases of no information, which could suggest that the child's previous record is not regarded as an important factor by the police.

The figures relating to behavioural factors are more clear-cut, but this is offset by the small numbers in some of the categories. In Bristol, for example, all cases of obstruction and 'other damage' were prosecuted, whereas hardly any of the cases of burglary or theft were taken to court. This is not, however, true of the Wiltshire population, where, besides obstruction and damage, burglary and theft have high prosecution rates. Unfortunately,

data on value of property damaged or stolen are not sufficiently available to elucidate these findings further.
Results for the two areas combined show that obstruction,
damage and burglary have high prosecution rates; theft,
ticket frauds and trespass moderate rates; and summary
offences are much more likely to be cautioned. A possible
factor in the number of NFA decisions is the presence of
children already in care, whom we know from the main study
to be protected from further prosecution.

As with cases processed by the 'civil' police the more
offences a child committed, the more likely he was to be
prosecuted. It would not be true to say that the same
phenomenon occurs with increasing number of children
involved in an event, but a 'snowball' pattern, as
opposed to what we have described as a 'group offence',
clearly carries a high risk of prosecution.

Reverting to the distinction previously drawn between
offences that are railway specific and those which are
not, there was a higher proportion of prosecutions for
non-railway offences, when the two areas are combined,
but this does not reach statistical significance. When
the figures for each area are looked at, however, we found
that in Wiltshire 'non-railway' offences carried a significantly higher risk of prosecution than railway-specific
offences, and that 'non-railway' offenders were significantly more likely to be prosecuted in Wiltshire than in
Bristol.

We have now described some of the ways in which the
police forces in Bristol and Wiltshire and the British
Transport Police set about deciding what to do with the
children who come to their attention for the commission
of offences. Those who are allocated to the 'no further
action' category are simply entered in police files.

Those children who are to be cautioned are contacted by
the police. In Bristol they are asked to attend the
central police station, together with one or both parents
in order to receive a formal caution. In Wiltshire some
children who live a long way from the nearest police
station may be cautioned by a senior officer who visits
them at home. In Bristol the caution is administered by
the head of the juvenile bureau, an inspector or his
deputy. The child and the parents are seen both separately and together, and left in no doubt as to the purpose
of the procedure; which is to warn the child against any
repetition of his offence behaviour. Although the
strength of the message can be varied to match the nature
of the offence or the perceived weaknesses of the individual child, its impact remains one of being 'told off'.
Children who are to be prosecuted and who are not already

in custody receive summonses to appear in the juvenile
court on a given date. The whole process, as we have now
described it, from the commission of an offence to the
administration of a caution or the first appearance in
court can take from less than twenty four hours to more
than a year.

The average length of time from first police contact
to the administration of a caution was 45 days in Wiltshire and 23 in Bristol. For offenders who were prosecuted the average period to first court hearing was 69 days
in Wiltshire and 36 in Bristol. No attempt has been made
to interpret the differences in timing which seem to mark
the operation of juvenile justice in the two areas
studied. There are no comparable data for other police
areas, and no national averages to act as a yardstick.
But however long it takes them to get there the children
who are sent summonses find themselves on the threshold of
yet another and even more complex decision-making process;
the juvenile court.

Chapter six

In court: Trial and sentence

Police decision-making takes place in private; part of an administrative process of considerable complexity. Juvenile courts sit, if not in public, then at least in a way which makes partly visible the routes by which they reach their decisions. Most importantly their proceedings require the presence of the accused juvenile and his or her parents, or guardians.

At one level the juvenile court is still a place of trial; a forum where facts are confirmed or found wanting. Its procedures have been designed and refined for the determination of guilt or innocence. In the adversary system of law these take the form of accusations followed by opportunities for rebuttal. Alternative accounts of what 'really happened' are presented to the judiciary for arbitration. In reaching and passing judgment, juries, judges and magistrates involve themselves in redefining reality, since whether they are right or mistaken about past events, their decisions create 'as-if' situations with a potentially profound influence on the future. A criminal conviction, depending on its seriousness, can significantly affect the life chances of an individual, drawing the attention of the police to his activities, increasing the chances of prosecution if he is caught again, and barring access to a number of careers. The need for judicial certainty therefore remains strong, even though the consequences of a wrong decision are less dire now than when sentences of hanging, flogging and transportation were still possible.

But just as a past conviction can have a pejorative meaning for a prospective employer, so in the same way, magistrates may make certain assumptions about the children the police choose to bring before them. Juvenile court chairmen in Bristol and Wiltshire for example estimated that their local police forces caught only a small proportion of all the children who actually commit offences. And two thirds of them were unwilling even to guess what proportions of the ones caught by the police were subsequently cautioned or prosecuted. For the most part they prefer to express confidence in the decisions made by the police and assume that the cases they see have been pre-selected for 'seriousness' or social difficulty. 'They (the police) only bring children they know', said one chairman of a rural court. 'And who have been found guilty in their opinion'. This kind of assumption has implications, as we shall see, for the sentencing pattern which prevails in the two areas, and probably elsewhere as well.

Another chairman, however, was alive to the dangers of allowing the police to make such a crucial decision. 'In practice it is right, in theory it is wrong because you are convicting somebody without trying them.' And the comment of another, that without police discretion 'courts would be inundated' identified a key issue. Courts simply deal with whatever cases come before them. But the police are responsible both for managing the flow of work into the courts and for stage-managing the 'factual' part of the legal proceedings. It is in their interests to make sure that the flow is not only smooth but also of a size that can be conveniently handled within the limits imposed by existing resources, especially those of scarce man-power. The growth in cautioning practices which has accompanied rising crime rates may be as much a means of controlling the volume of juvenile court business as it is a humanitarian gesture.

The semi-public nature of juvenile court proceedings also has implications for children and their parents. Despite the simplification of procedures, the juvenile court in action still retains the look and the feel of some of the dramatic ritual which dignifies adult justice. The drama, it was suggested earlier, is that of making manifest the otherwise disembodied values of justice, social control and welfare. The power of the State is often symbolized in the Royal Crest, set high up and in a central position behind the bench. The bench itself is raised a step or two above the level of the courtroom and the front of it is almost always totally enclosed, in contrast to the tables behind which other servants of the court sit. Defendants and their parents have no such aids to social ease within the courtroom. They sit on straightforward chairs or have to stand whilst being addressed by the court. The dramatic elements in this physical setting are sometimes heightened by the abrupt entries and departures of the magistrates, to the

accompaniment of loud commands to rise or 'be seated'.
These are uttered in many courts by the ushers who play a
considerable part in the proceedings. They are responsible for procuring the appearance in the courtroom of
individual children on the list, at the right time, in
the same order as they appear on collective charge sheets,
and with the appropriate parents standing behind them.

The way in which all this is achieved makes an important contribution to the climate of the courtroom. Some
ushers perform their duties in a physical and peremptory
fashion; pushing and pulling the children and their
parents into position. Others do what has to be done
with courtesy and dignity. They are also charged with
maintaining good order, although some of them are elderly
and probably not capable of dealing with more than verbal
or procedural misdemeanours. They can however guard
against intrusions of human emotion. If a mother bursts
into tears the usher will remonstrate comfortingly, or
offer a glass of water or a chair to sit on. Dealing with
noises off in the corridors or waiting room, children
crying or loud conversation will be his responsibility as
well. In some courts it is the usher's job to administer
the oath, and since he usually wears long black robes he
must appear to children as a semi-sacred and important
person.

In most of the courts we observed, little apparent
effort was made to acquaint the children and their parents
with the identities of all the officials present. In
Bristol that would have been a considerable chore because
the number of participants was never less than about
twenty. In one Wiltshire court where pressure of business
was less, the chairman made a point of introducing every
person in the room and explaining the functions of those
involved in the case. This took some time but appeared
to reassure the parents and to some extent the children.

Physically, apart from symbolizing the majesty of law,
juvenile courtrooms tend to be arranged so as to allow for
two simultaneous confrontations. The primary one is that
between the child and the bench. The other is between
the police who prosecute and any defence representatives
who may be present. In most cases there is no legal rep-
resentative for the defence and the configuration is a
triangular one; bench, police, child. In the child-bench
confrontation, nothing is allowed to obscure any part of
the accused from the gaze of the magistrates, although
they are protected, to some extent by the bench, from his.
Being looked at or stared at, simply being the centre of
attention, is a painful business for most people. Children are even less habituated to it than adults, and the

stress is intensified by the adverse circumstances that
give rise to it in court. Magistrates often raise and
lower their eyes in unison to scrutinize the children in
front of them. They peer at his face when the charge is
read and he makes his plea. And there is obvious concern,
on the part of the court, with the actual appearance of
some defendants. The initial interaction in a few cases
we observed was devoted to suspected smirking or sweet-
sucking and gum-chewing by children. Together with the
usher's attention to placing and posture this emphasis on
oral discipline seems to serve two purposes. One is to
establish the court and its procedures as the exclusive
frame of reference for all the participants. The second
is to emphasize, especially to those making first appearances in court, that they are like players in a game who
must pick up the rules as they go along, often by
breaking them.

Unrepresented first-timers and their parents are at a
decided disadvantage in following and influencing court
proceedings. It is unlikely that many of them will have
been briefed by anybody about what to expect. There is
no widely available consumer's handbook to the juvenile
court, and although clerks and chairmen may be considerate
little real help will be offered during the actual hearing
of the case. After routine name-taking and a query about
the age of the child, the first hurdle is the plea.
Although a simplified form of charge is read out by the
Clerk to the Court, some defendants seem to experience
difficulty in framing a legally acceptable reply to the
question 'Do you admit that?' The problem lies in the
starkness of the options between which they must choose.
If the accused wishes to introduce the question of motive,
it must seem logical to him to do it when the charge is
put. Technically he is expected to deny the charge in
such circumstances, but it can take time to get there as
this dialogue shows.

Clerk:	You are charged with taking without the owner's consent a motor scooter on the 20th of January for your own use. Do you admit or deny?
Boy:	I want a word to explain.
Clerk:	You agree that you took the vehicle.
Boy:	It didn't work. It wouldn't go, like.
Clerk:	You drove the motor scooter on the road. Have you a driving licence?
Boy:	I was in a rush and I just didn't remember it.
Police:	He was saying that he thought it had been abandoned. In those circumstances I think he should plead 'not guilty'.

Magistrate: Stand up. The court is in some little diffic-
              ulty as to whether you are pleading guilty or
              not to this offence. You have said on a
              previous occasion that you thought this
              vehicle had been abandoned and therefore the
              implication of that. Was it in bad condition?
              Was it usable?
Boy: Not really.
Magistrate: Did you get it going within a few minutes?
Boy: I pushed it. I ran it down the street and
              then the policeman saw me.
Clerk: Are you saying at the time of the taking you
              thought it was abandoned?
Boy: I saw it there for a couple of Sundays. I
              saw it lying against this fence. There was a
              lot of parts loose.
Magistrate: What you are now saying is that you have not
              committed the offence with which you are
              charged.
Father: He took the bike away. He saw the bike and
              there was a 15 day lapse. It was not con-
              cealed in any way.
Magistrate: We treat this as 'not guilty'. The court
              directs that a plea of 'not guilty' be entered
              and we will make up our minds about that.
              Have you any witnesses?

The tension between the legal requirement for a 'yes-
no' response to the charge, the boy's determination to
give a qualified answer, and the magistrate's anxiety to
do the right thing by the defendant, emerges graphically
here. But however hard benches try, they find it impossible to keep out all legal language. Both the boy and
his father in this case were exceptionally able to
express themselves. In most cases a resigned acquies-
cence lubricates the smooth passage of the plea-taking.

The artificiality of court dialogue and the esoteric
nature of some of the conventions governing the giving of
evidence were also illustrated during the hearing of a
contested care application being made by a local authority. In this case it was the senior social worker who
lacked judicial experience. First, she flouted the rules
by remaining in the room during previous testimony. As a
witness she persisted in repeating 'hearsay' evidence.
And she failed to master the trick of listening to
questions from one direction (the defence lawyer) and
giving answers in another (towards the bench). The chairman of the court warned her twice and then expressed
public criticisms of the shortcomings of social workers
in court proceedings.

A tiny minority of juveniles do possess the social
skills and the confidence to contribute verbally; like
the boy who re-appeared before a bench after a three-week
remand in custody:

'Well', said the magistrate, looking up from the
assessment centre report, 'You don't seem to have been
working to your full potential.'

'The full potential down there', replied the boy, 'is
digging the garden.'

On other occasions the terminology employed by court
personnel, and by implication the proceedings themselves,
seem to have little or no meaning for the children. As
when the chairman asked a girl during care proceedings:

'It is said that you are exposed to moral danger. Is
that true?'

The girl replied, truthfully no doubt, 'I don't know.'

In crime cases the language is less likely to be mis-
construed and the first part of the procedure is relatively straightforward. After identification and plea
have taken place, the police case is presented by an
inspector, sometimes in uniform, sometimes in civilian
dress. He or she is unknown to the child and the parents;
the officer who made the original investigation will
appear only if there is a plea of not guilty. Police
evidence is economically brief and crisply delivered. It
starts with a recital of the case summary made by the
investigating officer. Although the prosecution case
normally rests on more work than any other report produced in court, its presentation generally takes least
time.

When the police case has been presented and the facts
have been 'found' magistrates often ask supplementary
questions about the offence events and invite comments
from the juvenile. A typical opening in such exchanges
is a neutral 'Is there anything you wish to say?' Most
children say nothing or mutter inaudibly at this point.
A few express conventional regret: 'I'm sorry I did it,
and for all the trouble I've caused. It won't happen
again.' If there is no reply or an attempted justification is made, the bench may openly request that contrition
be shown.

In a case of urinating in the street for example, the
court chairman asked one of the boys involved: 'Is there
anything you wish to say?'

The boy replied 'I am a stranger here. I didn't know
where the toilets were.'

Magistrate: 'It is an indecent act and an unpleasant
thing to do. Do you regret it?' Receiving no reply, the
chairman turned to the other boy, who excused himself in

similar terms, adding 'There are not enough signs to the toilet.'

'We', said the chairman, 'are better off than most towns of this size. There are various places.' Then, having failed to elicit any signs of remorse, and having countered, as he saw it, their defence, he proceeded to draw the morals. First a private one: 'It is up to you to control yourself a little better isn't it? We are all alike.' And then a public one: 'We are getting rather a lot of this happening in the town. It is a beastly habit. It can be avoided if you only think about these things. It is most unpleasant for the shop-keepers and householders, and one we mean to stamp out.'

Magistrates also pursue the personal dimensions of offence behaviour in two further ways. First by asking for explanations. 'Why did you do this?' is asked so frequently and receives so few replies that its use seems at first sight to be merely rhetorical. But there is a serious purpose to be discovered behind it. The 'causes' of criminal behaviour are often discussed in the reports submitted by probation officers and social workers, but magistrates also appear to be genuinely in search of explanations direct from the horse's mouth.

Second some magistrates seem keen to use the court appearance, not just as an occasion for censure, but as a learning opportunity. In traffic cases particularly they try to use the proceedings as a kind of consequential education. 'You didn't realise it was serious', said one chairman to a boy accused of ignoring a no-entry sign, 'coming along that side of the motorway?'

'It was foggy', replied the boy, 'but it could have been very serious.'

Or:

'I do appreciate that boys enjoy motor cycles, but you must realise the danger to yourself and to others. Somewhere off the main road is the best place to learn. You could have caused an accident with other people.'

The optimum response to this kind of remark is one of grateful insight into the possibilities of danger and damage to others. Remarkably few of the traffic offences did involve injury or damage, and the appeal must therefore be to what might have been. In property offences, by contrast, the impact on others is typically interpreted back to the culprit in these terms:

'How would you like it if someone came into your home and took your money or bicycle?' To which, of course, there is no answer. Parents too are asked if there is anything they wish to say. A standard answer is that 'he is a good boy at home' and that his bad behaviour outside

must be a consequence of his mixing with undesirable
peers. Occasionally a father claims to have 'disciplined'
the child 'in his own way' for the offence. Magistrates
usually want to know what this means and appear to be
relieved when it turns out to be loss of pocket money, or
being kept in, rather than a beating.

When the child or the parents have finished what they
wish to say the magistrates must begin the process of
deciding what sentence to impose. Trial is a narrow and
precise function which can call on the more exact of the
forensic sciences for support. Sentencing is a much more
artistic activity. And whilst trial proceeds by the
strict exclusion of material, sentencing encourages its
widest possible inclusion. The chief sources of this
information in the juvenile court are the police who provide a list of any previous court appearances, schools
which systematically send reports on past or current
pupils, the school welfare service which deals with the
attendance record of the child, probation officers, local
authority social workers, child guidance clinic psychiatrists, and assessment centre staff. The school report
is the only one of these which is available in practically
every case.

No precise content analysis of the reports was carried
out in the present study but a reading of several hundred
of each of the major types leaves a distinctive impression of their language and contents. School reports are
invariably signed by head teachers but the actual author-
ship of the comments clearly varies from teachers who
appear to know the child extremely well to those who find
it difficult to say anything either positive or negative
about him. 'It seems to me', wrote one headmaster, 'that
the main causal factor in this boy's fall from grace
arises within his own rather dull personality.' The
general tenor of the remarks in school reports is a persistently negative one. Occasionally 'keen', 'polite' or
'helpful' boys surprise their teachers by 'getting involved in this kind of behaviour'. Mostly though, the
offenders seem to be portrayed as 'below average', 'capable of better work', 'not living up to earlier promise'
or as being 'bullies' or characterized by 'downright low
cunning'. Many of these judgments exceed in censorious-
ness those made by all the other reporting groups. Police
files, for example, betray a concern with such things as
discipline in the home, or the influence of delinquent
companions , but in tone they are closer to what social
workers say than they are to teachers. Probation officers
submit court reports to a more predictable format than do
local authority social workers. They appear to dwell more

on the concrete details of the offender's environment than
the social workers who sometimes pay greater attention to
the early history of the child and to the 'dynamics' of
the family situation.

The 1933 Children and Young Persons Act laid a duty on
local authorities to provide information on children
appearing in court 'except in cases which appear to them
to be of a trivial nature'. Section 9.1 of the 1969 Act
reiterates this duty but replaces the reference to triviality with the phrase 'unless they are of opinion that
it is unnecessary to do so'. Since one of the major aims
of the 1969 legislation was to keep children out of court
so far as possible it seems reasonable to assume that
when juvenile offenders are prosecuted, it is either
because they have committed 'serious' crimes, or because
they are in need of some treatment measure which lies
within the power of the court. Either way it might be
expected that social enquiry reports (SERs) would be
available to the magistrates in a very high proportion of
the cases they deal with. We found that one third of the
145 juvenile court cases we studied in Wiltshire, and one
quarter of the 143 Bristol cases were adjudicated without
SERs. These totals refer to non-traffic offenders only.
Traffic cases in court hardly ever attract social work
interest and only 5 SERs were submitted for the 114
traffic offenders in our study population. The probation
service provided reports on about half the children
appearing in court in both areas, but the social services
department in Wiltshire dealt with less than half as many
as their colleagues in Bristol (12 per cent compared to
26 per cent). And in Wiltshire both the probation
officers and the social workers appeared more reticent to
make firm recommendations to the bench than their Bristol
counterparts. Nearly 90 per cent of the Bristol reports
ended with firm conclusions; just over 50 per cent of the
Wiltshire ones did so. When interviewed, Wiltshire juvenile court chairmen claimed to welcome positive recommendations and there is no immediately obvious reason for
this finding.

Supervision orders, not surprisingly, were the most
frequently made recommendations, accounting for around a
third of the totals in the two counties. The Bristol
magistrates accepted and implemented over 90 per cent of
the recommendations for supervision, but in Wiltshire,
where fewer firm conclusions were submitted, the equivalent figure was 50 per cent.

But the reverse is the case for care orders, where the
Bristol benches rejected one in three of the care recommendations made by probation officers or social workers.

This evidence suggests that juvenile magistrates, although they welcome the fullest information possible on the children before them, retain a considerable independence in actually reaching their decisions.

The decisions they did make can be seen in the totals to Table 6.1.

TABLE 6.1   Children who went to court: court outcome

	BRISTOL	WILTSHIRE
	%	%
Borstal	1 (0.7)	2 (1.4)
Detention centre	3 (2.1)	3 (2.1)
Attendance centre	18 (12.6)	0
Fine	37 (25.9)	65 (44.8)
Care order	15 (10.5)	20 (13.8)
Sup. order (Probation)	31 (21.7)	31 (21.4)
Supervision order (LA)	13 (9.1)	5 (3.4)
Remit other court	2 (1.4)	5 (3.4)
Adjourned sine die	1 (0.7)	1 (0.7)
Conditional discharge	19 (13.3)	6 (4.1)
Absolute discharge	1 (0.7)	0
Not guilty	1 (0.7)	1 (0.7)
Dismissed, charge withdrawn	1 (0.7)	6 (4.1)
Total	143 (100)	145 (100)

In Bristol there is a rough balance between supervision orders (31 per cent) and fines (26 per cent). In Wiltshire fines outstrip all other dispositions, accounting for 43 per cent of all the court decisions. But the gap between the two benches narrows when allowance is made for the availability of an attendance centre in Bristol. Thirteen per cent of the children who appeared in Bristol juvenile court were given attendance centre orders, and if they are added to those who were fined, the total is not far short of the Wiltshire figure for fines alone. If discharges, supervision orders and care orders are seen as 'helpful' in intent, and fines, attendance centre orders and committals to detention centres or Borstals are seen

as penalties, then the courtroom population in both areas
divides into two roughly equal-sized groups. One half is
'helped', the other penalized. It neatly illustrates the
tension that exists between the basically inassimilable
aims of the juvenile court - to dispense justice whilst
at the same time promoting the welfare of children.

Numbers are small, but in Bristol the use of penalties
appears to be associated with age, current offence and
previous record. The influence of age on court disposition follows the three-part pattern discerned in the discussion of police decisions. The under 13s receive
'treatment' sentences, and the sixteen-year-olds are
penalized. Between thirteen and fifteen the conditional
discharges are more frequently imposed and a general balance between the types of disposition is struck.

The Wiltshire figures show the same progression for the
three age ranges. These results may be partly due to the
greater criminal experience of the older boys and to the
types of offence they tend to commit; such as TWOC and
summary offences. But contrary to the expectation that
more serious and more recidivist offenders are increasingly at risk of being placed in care, the sixteen-year-
olds who answer this description are less likely to be
dealt with in that way. Boys in this position may have
already exhausted the short tariff system of the juvenile
court, but they have also reached an age where its sanctions carry less and less conviction. For between a care
order and a committal for Borstal sentence or even a
detention centre order there is a gap which only the most
serious and persistent kind of delinquency can bridge.
The result is that some sixteen-year-olds appear to enjoy
a relative immunity from the custodial consequences of
their behaviour.

One curious feature of dispositions in both areas is
the neglect of 'absolute discharge'. Magistrates often
plead for extensions to the range of sentencing options
open to them. And yet only 1 order of 'absolute discharge' was made out of 288 cases in the two areas. Conditional discharge too was little used in Wiltshire (only
4.1 per cent of all decisions compared with 13.3 per cent
in Bristol). Courts may feel, possibly because of the
terminology itself, that an 'absolute discharge' is not
only limited in its impact on the offender, but is a kind
of studied insult to the police who decided that the case
was worth prosecuting in the first instance.

The small numbers of children appearing in court in
this study preclude a more detailed analysis of other
factors which may be associated with magistrates' decisions, but it is possible to check what they do in

relation to groups of offenders. Thirty-three groups of
offenders appeared together in the juvenile court in
Bristol within the study period. In 10 of them, all the
members received the same disposition, and in the remaining 23 they were split between different sentencing
options. Wiltshire courts dealt with 32 groups, 20 of
them in the same way and 12 differently. Although the
proportions of split groups are much higher in the juvenile court than in the police decision-making process,
there is still, in Wiltshire, at any rate, a tendency to
treat all the members of a delinquent group in the same
way.

A number of railway offenders were also dealt with in
court; 30 of them in Bristol and 22 in Wiltshire. Of the
Bristol children, 10 were fined, 9 conditionally dis-
charged and 7 given supervision orders. In the Wiltshire
courts, 18 of the railway offenders were fined and 4
placed under supervision. All but one of the Wiltshire
children were dealt with in one court appearance, but in
Bristol over a third needed two or three appearances. As
with the main study, we found that numbers of children
were dealt with in court without a social enquiry report;
we could not trace an SER in the records for two thirds
of the Bristol railway children and one third of those
from Wiltshire.

In Bristol conditional discharges were favoured for
those children who were younger and who had committed the
offence of trespass, whether or not they had had previous
court appearances. The supervision orders also tended to
be given to offenders aged fourteen or under, and to
children who had not appeared previously. Eight out of
the ten fines were given to the sixteen-year-olds. The
one attendance centre order was given to a child with a
previous court record. The Wiltshire magistrates, as we
found in the main study, made predominant use of the fine,
and without more detailed information about individual
cases than we were able to record it is not possible to
make any worthwhile comments on the decisions they made.
It is interesting that, in both areas, fines were imposed
on the ten- to twelve-year-old railway children, a marked
departure from the practice with the offenders in the
main study.

Finally, all the traffic offenders who appeared
in court were dealt with as though they constituted one
large group, and all but 5 out of 114 were fined. It
provides final confirmation for the existence of what
might be called the 'traffic paradox' by which young
traffic offenders are processed through the juvenile
justice system in a completely different way to children

who commit offences involving dishonesty or damage or
violence. When the practitioners in our interview population were asked 'Are traffic offenders as much in need of
help as other juvenile offenders?' less than a quarter of
them thought that they were. The rest considered that
the commission of traffic offences did not merit social
work investigation since the children involved were
unlikely to have personal difficulties requiring outside
help. Not one of them expressed any curiosity at the
sharp distinctions which are drawn between the two groups
of offenders.

So far as traffic cases are concerned the whole debate
about criminal responsibility, relief from stigma and the
desirability of making court decisions in the best interests of the child might never have occurred. Ingleby,
Longford and Kilbrandon all ignored the question as did
the two White Papers, the Bill and the 1969 Act itself.

Chapter seven

'The interests of the child':
Past, present and future

More than a century of social inquiry has revealed a top-
ography of crime which is dominated by a number of monu-
mental features. The most important of them can be
summarized in the statement that most detected crime is
committed by small groups of young urban working-class
males. A host of less well attested details dot the land-
scape around these massive central 'facts'. Criminologists in search of the causes of crime have tended to
address themselves to the larger issues in terms which
reflect the intellectual concerns of their times.
Lombroso derived his ideas of genetic atavism from
Darwin. Psychoanalytic thought has had a major influence
on theories about the aetiology of individual delinquent
behaviour. And more recent theorists have stressed the
wider social factors involved. All three approaches have
adopted a basically determinist position, even though
their conclusions and their prescriptions for action have
taken radically different forms. A parallel and volum-
inous tradition of empirical research has eschewed explicit theory altogether. Since such work tends to
accept the current situation as given, it follows that
its implications for policy fall almost unfailingly into
the deepest ruts of incremental pragmatism.

One way of interpreting the findings of this study
would be to engage in a detailed critique of the defects
of the 1969 Children and Young Persons Act in practice.
They could be used to make a case for continuing to
strengthen and improve consultation procedures between
the police and the social services departments; or for
the provision of more social enquiry reports to the
courts. The police might be persuaded to examine their
use of the 'no further action' decision and steps taken
to include it in the annual criminal statistics. They
might be interested in extending their data collection in

the direction of more welfare-related items or in looking
at some of the differences which appear to exist between
some of their decision-makers. More consideration might
be urged for traffic offenders than is presently the case.
Magistrates might be encouraged to make more use of the
absolute discharge. But some of our findings would fit
uneasily into such a framework. Some of them suggest the
need for a far more fundamental re-appraisal of the underlying concepts of juvenile justice.

In the historical discussion in chapter 1 the development of child-law in England and Wales was related to the
construction of what was termed a 'moral quarantine'.
This was defined as the period between the minimum age of
responsibility as legally expressed and the age at which
children were thought fit to assume full public accountability for their actions.

Its boundaries are those of the juvenile court jurisdiction, and its contents rest on some vital assumptions
about 'children in trouble'. The first of them is that
child offenders are qualitatively different from adult
ones. Initially the difference was seen as an innocence
that had to be protected from corruption. Later it
became an assertion that children who steal are the same
as children who are deprived of proper parental care. On
that basis punishment for offences was increasingly construed as inappropriate and in need of replacement by
individualized 'treatment' measures. The movement within
which these changes took place was characterized as an
attempted fusion between the ideas of justice on the one
hand and of welfare on the other.

The proceedings of the Longford Committee and the long
struggle over its proposals led to the passing of an Act
in 1969 which embodied the divided state of professional
and public opinion over the extent to which this process
of fusion should be continued. In Scotland, where the
juvenile court had never really taken root, the 1968
Social Work (Scotland) Act had leap-frogged the contemporary debate in England and established a system for
dealing with children in trouble which was nearer to a
Scandinavian welfare-based model than to a due-process
one. The outcome of the legal changes in England, though
less dramatic, was broadly in the same direction.
Although the criminal sanction was retained, an informal
emphasis was placed on keeping children out of court as
far as possible. Police decision-making was to be made
more sensitive to the 'interests of the child' by the
views of social workers. And more power was given to
social workers to undertake treatment activities with
children who had come to court.

Even so it fell far short of what the reformers had
wanted and it produced a system which appears to combine
the worst of all possible worlds, and in a way that satis-
fies none of the protagonists in the justice versus welfare debate. It is neither a judicial system with a
clear mandate to protect the interests of society; nor a
welfare one with an untrammeled remit to cherish the
children it encounters. Some of the conceptual and
organizational dilemmas which this failed fusion of opposites poses to policemen, social workers and magistrates
were spelt out in chapter 2. And some of its practical
consequences were reported in chapters 3 to 6. They
depict, more clearly than might have been expected, a
system in which major decisions about children are made
primarily on the basis of how old they are and what they
have done rather than on some assessment of their personal
needs. Our findings that police decisions, and to a
lesser extent those made in court, are distinctively
related to three age groups is critical in this respect.
It may be tentatively explained as follows.

The age of responsibility has always represented a conservative estimate of the moral awareness of children.
Many of the practitioners we interviewed thought that
children appreciated right and wrong from a much earlier
age than ten. But very few of them wished to see the
present age of responsibility lowered towards what they
saw as the reality of the situation. Nor did many of them
wish to see the age raised to any significant extent. The
present age seemed, in other words, to be 'about right'.
Policemen gave verbal support to this view but suited
their actions to a different kind of principle. In the
years immediately prior to the passing of the 1963
Children and Young Persons Act there had been a decline
in the absolute number of prosecutions of children aged
eight to ten. In the context of a generally rising rate
of juvenile crime these figures suggest a growing reluc-
tance on the part of the police to bring children of that
age group before the courts. The raising of the age of
responsibility to ten in 1964 has been followed by a similar phenomenon affecting ten- to twelve-year-old offenders; a process which has been further reinforced by the
advent of the 1969 Act. During the same period there
has been no corresponding increase in the numbers of
children of those ages appearing in the juvenile courts
purely on care grounds. It is possible, but not very
likely, that these younger children are now being super-
vized on an informal basis by social services departments.
What is more probable is that the children have disappeared entirely from official view through a trap-door

of 'benign neglect'. The practical effect of this police
action has been to establish what amounts to a de facto
age of criminal responsibility at twelve. It can only be
a matter for speculation; but it may be that one of the
reasons why policemen allow a generous margin beyond the
minimum age of responsibility is in order to avoid difficult decisions which involve children who commit offences
with companions who are below the age of ten.

Our data do suggest that this is an important factor
at the other end of the juvenile court age range. More
than half of the fifteen- and sixteen-year-old boys were
found to commit offences with older youths who came
within the jurisdiction of the adult criminal court. And
the older children constituted the third group which we
distinguished in our analysis of police and court
decisions. Whereas the under twelves were hardly ever
prosecuted and were given mainly 'treatment' dispositions
in court if they appeared there, the older children were
dealt with by all the agencies almost as though they were
already adults. They were prosecuted more frequently than
other juveniles and when they appeared in court were given
fewer treatment sentences. The two discontinuities in the
graphs of prosecution by age circumscribe an intermediate
age band within which the children appear to receive that
blend of justice and welfare which the 1969 Act presumably intended for all juveniles. Policemen and courts
appear to resolve the dilemmas posed by the arbitrary age
limits of the 'moral quarantine' in a way which limits
the application of the 'spirit of the Act' to no more
than a half of the original target population. If our
findings were restricted to Bristol and Wiltshire alone
they would have little wider significance, but there is
some support from other studies for the idea that a
middle age group of children, the equivalents of the
plateau years in our graphs, are dealt with in a distinctive way by the police and the courts.(1) One interpretation of this finding therefore is that it identifies a
major structural flaw in the whole argument for a separate
juvenile jurisdiction. If, for whatever reasons, the system can deliver what it sees as an appropriate service to
only one half of its designated clientele the need for a
review of its basic format appears to be self-evident.

Three other findings from our research support this
contention. The first of them is the limited number of
behavioural factors which appear to determine police
decisions. It could be argued that the relatively undeveloped state of consultation at the time of our study
accounts for this, but even in Bristol where the specialist officers of the juvenile bureau made intensive efforts

to contact social workers about offenders already known
to them, our data do not indicate that factors related to
the personal needs of the children played any significant
part in determining the final decisions. The design of
police paperwork and the attitudes of officers also betray
a deep-seated concern with the overt behaviour of children, and hence with its degree of offensiveness. It may
be that in time a more child-centred approach would 'rub
off' on the police through contact with social workers in
an increasingly effective process of consultation. But
there is an equal likelihood that the influence could be
in the opposite direction, and that social workers might
become more control-minded instead. At the court stage
too there is evidence that magistrates divide the children
who come before them into two roughly equal-sized groups;
one of which they help, and the other they penalize. In
reaching their decisions the courts do not accept uncrit-
ically what social workers and probation officers recommend to them in their social enquiry reports.

Both the police and the courts therefore appear to give
a degree of priority to the public protection aspect of
their work with children. Social workers left to themselves might perhaps arrive at more child-centred solutions. That is not a criticism of either the police or
the courts but a pointer perhaps to the impossibility of
ever reaching, within the current arrangements, the kind of
treatment for 'children in trouble' to which reformers
like Lord Longford have aspired.

A second and related finding concerns the unwillingness
of the police to split between different dispositions
groups of children who commit the same offences. If the
interests of the individual child were at the forefront of
the policeman's mind when he made these decisions, groups
of offenders in which all the members were dealt with in
the same way would be in a considerable minority. The
fact that they are not may be due to firmly held notions
of natural justice which are affronted by the differential
treatment of delinquents who have been caught for doing
the same thing. Feelings like this are probably shared
by the children and families involved and the difficulty
of interpreting such decisions to irate parents may well
reinforce the initial aversion of the police to the practice. Whatever the causes, these facts lend added
strength to an emerging picture of an unsound system of
juvenile justice.

And third the traffic offenders drive a metaphorical
horse-and-cart through the case for a separate juvenile
court. For they constitute an entire behavioural category
of child offenders which is almost wholly ignored both by

the special philosophy and the welfare oriented practices
of the juvenile jurisdiction.

They are excluded from consultation procedures; they
are prosecuted almost as often as they would be if they
were adults and more often than most other juveniles.
They are not given the 'benefit' of social enquiry reports
in court, and they are sentenced primarily in respect of
their behaviour, which is thought to merit a financial
penalty in virtually every case. People who work in the
system draw a sharp distinction between traffic offenders
and other children, claiming that they are not usually in
need of the social inquiries and offers of help which
mark the official response to other kinds of youthful deviance. This belief is not based on any kind of evidence
since it precedes and therefore precludes the very activity that would provide it. But it may well draw on a
widespread conviction that an appearance in court on a
traffic charge does not carry the same degree of stigma
as one for more criminal offences such as theft or
assault. From the standpoint of the offender, however,
the only real difference in the courtroom experiences of
the two types of offender lies in the wholly punitive
nature of the sentences awarded to the traffic cases.
And in the possibility that the bench will regard the
traffic offender as more responsible for his behaviour
than other children and more suitable for a 'telling off'.
The fact is that traffic offenders have slipped through
the net of all the efforts to infuse the juvenile court
with the ethos of a social welfare agency.

The pragmatic response to these criticisms would be to
patch and darn the present fabric of juvenile justice into
some semblance of reasonable repair. But persisting criticisms by magistrates and others, and the unlikelihood in
the present economic climate of securing substantial new
resources to bolster up the system suggest that now is
the time to consider how it might be ordered differently.
Our own conviction, based on these research results, and
on three years close acquaintance with the system at work
is that the juvenile court idea has been tried and found
wanting, and that it suffers from congenital defects
which fresh applications of money or manpower would any-
how fail to cure. We recommend accordingly that the
attempt to fuse justice with welfare be abandoned and that
the juvenile court as such should disappear.

It can be replaced in any of a number of ways which
need not reproduce either of its principal drawbacks;
namely the confusion of help with punishment; and the
self-defeating limitations imposed by an age-based jurisdiction. Some specific proposals are made here which are

claimed to be neither definitive nor exhaustive; but they
are compatible with our analysis of the system in operation.

If the separate strands of child care and justice were
to be disentangled from the juvenile court jurisdiction,
two distinct populations of children would require to be
provided for; those in need of care or protection, and
those who commit offences. There is an obvious overlap
in membership between these two groups but our limited
findings suggest that it may have been exaggerated in the
past for the not unworthy motive of protecting children
from the full weight of the criminal law. Where it still
exists it might cause some difficulty for some of the procedures we are proposing, but the numbers involved are so
small that they do not justify the creation of a special
system to meet their particular needs.

For the children who are suffering from parental neglect, who are in moral danger or who are not attending
school we suggest that a separate care jurisdiction could
be set up. Many of the present juvenile court panel
members might find this an attractive jurisdiction in
which to work. A separate care court would also be an
obvious candidate for incorporation in a family court
system. Indeed a family court without a care jurisdiction
is as much of a conceptual nonsense as the juvenile court
has been with it. A second major advantage would also
accrue from the separation of the care and crime jurisdictions of the juvenile court. If social workers did
not have to divide their attention between the demands of
social protection and the needs of the individual child,
they could concentrate on providing a committed and child-
centred service to families at risk. Within the framework of an inclusive family court it might even be possible for social services departments to regain some of
the single-mindedness, now lost, which marked the pre-
Seebohm Children's Departments. In one way the future of
children in need of care and protection is not difficult
to resolve, since they are so few in number and their
problems clearly delimited. There is however one complic-
ation. Under the original formulation of the 1969
Children and Young Persons Act, the commission of an
offence was to have become one more ground on which, provided that the care condition was also fulfilled, care
proceedings could be brought in the juvenile court. It
is our view that a new and separate care jurisdiction
within the family court should not have any dealings what-
soever with children as offenders, but only with children
in need of care and protection. It is the confusion
between these two categories which has led to the present

situation. The answer to the problem does not lie in
persevering with the confusion but in ending it.

Juvenile offenders on the other hand pose more difficult problems. The present system fails to satisfy reformers who think that children should not be held fully
accountable for their actions and subsequently punished
for them. Other critics of the 1969 Act believe that the
present dispensation is too 'soft' on young offenders,
and does too little to protect society from the behaviour
of persistent or serious delinquents. The issue which
divides them is the age at which criminal responsibility
should commence. Reformers wish to raise it. Public
opinion and political realities indicate that there are
insurmountable barriers in the way of any substantial
advances in that direction. Our findings suggest one
possible solution to the dilemma. In terms of the
decisions made by police and magistrates, the two break
points in the age graphs, thirteen and fifteen in Bristol,
twelve and fourteen in Wiltshire, represent naturally
occurring locations for a possible new age of responsibility. If the age of responsibility were now to be
raised to twelve, it would simply give official recog-
nition to the de facto situation already described. Consideration might be given therefore to fixing a new
minimum age for prosecution somewhere around the fourteen-
to fifteen-year mark. This comes tantalisingly close to
the school-leaving age which has such obvious attractions
to reformers who would like to see the two legal limits
coincide and reinforce one another.

Our data indicate however that although official
decisions may distinguish sharply between younger and
older offenders, the distinctions do not show a neat
correspondence with school-leaving age. If the age of
responsibility were to be set at fourteen or fifteen
there is no reason to suppose that children who had only
recently qualified for prosecution would not, as now,
receive the benefit of the doubt from official decision-
makers, and be cautioned in considerable numbers. For
the children over that age who are prosecuted there is
little point in retaining a juvenile jurisdiction which
runs for only a further two or three years. Nor is there
any real justification for resurrecting the youth courts
proposed in the Longford Report, which would simply
repeat the contradictions of the 'moral quarantine' only
for an older age group. It would make better sense to
deal with fifteen- and sixteen-year-old offenders as
adults and to try and sentence them in the ordinary criminal and traffic jurisdictions of the adult magistrates
court. One safeguard might be added to the adult

proceedings, which is that the court could order the names or other identifying facts concerning any defendant under the age of twenty one to be withheld from press reports of the case in court.

For children under the age of fourteen or fifteen who commit offences it is not suggested that no official action be taken. For the typical minor juvenile offender the experience of being caught, supplemented by either an informal or a formal police caution would be a sufficient response. If however the apprehended offender showed signs of parental neglect the case could be referred to social services departments, as eight- and nine-year-olds now can be, for inquiry and if necessary voluntary supervision. If sufficiently clear-cut care conditions existed in the child's home circumstances then proceedings could be instituted in the care jurisdiction of the family court. If such conditions were not present, but the offence behaviour of the under-age child was such as to constitute a serious threat to the safety or well-being of other people then a new kind of public protection proceedings could be instituted possibly in the Crown Court. The aim of such proceedings would be to secure the detention of the child, not necessarily in his own interests, but in those of public safety. A protective custody order would commit the child to the kind of secure accommodation which Regional Planning Committees have proposed as part of the residential provision required under the present Act. The order would be for a finite period and could be appealed or reviewed at three monthly intervals. Such orders might seem to the child lobby to be retrogressive and punitive but faced with the current conjunction of public demands for protection and the lack of residential facilities it is almost inevitable that similar sentences will soon take place under the guise of care orders.

These proposals present the broad outline of one possible solution to the seemingly intractable problems of administering a system of juvenile justice which is based on irreconcilable principles and unrealistic requirements for scarce resources. They do not deal in detail with every possible difficulty or exceptional case that might arise in any attempt to implement them. And they leave open two very important questions; where should the new minimum age of responsibility be fixed? And what should be done with the older children who would appear in the adult magistrates court? We have made suggestions about the age of responsibility which can be supported from our findings. The sentencing of the older children in an adult jurisdiction, if it followed the current pattern to

be seen in the juvenile courts, would consist principally
of fines, some probation orders and a limited number of
orders committing boys to detention centres or to Crown
Court for Borstal sentences. But innovations in this area
would have to be tied in with any reforms which might
ensue from the 1974 report of the Younger Committee on
Young Adult Offenders.(2)

Finally our proposals would entail the disappearance of
the juvenile courts as such, which was also the goal of
the Longford Committee. Their ambition stemmed from an
impatience and a dissatisfaction with the operation of the
juvenile court. Our view is that the juvenile court idea
has made an historically invaluable contribution to the
tempering of justice with concern for the individual
offender. In 1908 it was necessary to split the children
off from the mainstream of the judicial process in order
to achieve this. Now that the principle has spread in
large measure to the adult jurisdiction as well there
seems to be no good reason why the older children should
not be returned there, and no good reason to suppose that
their interests will suffer as a consequence.

Appendix

Background to the study: Origins and methods

In 1971 the Home Office commissioned the University of
Bristol Department of Social Administration and Social
Work to conduct a study of the operation of Part I of the
Children and Young Persons Act, 1969. Responsibility for
Part II rests with the Department of Health and Social
Security and they arranged separately for the operation
of their portion of the legislation to be examined. It
is, therefore, important to be clear about the nature of
this division and the consequent limits imposed upon this
particular study.

We were not asked to describe or evaluate what happened
to children and young persons as a result of the decisions
made by the juvenile court; nor were we asked to consider
the organizational repercussions of the new legislation
upon local social services departments. These matters
were, and still are, largely the concern of the DHSS.

Even so, some of the decisions available to the juvenile courts in criminal proceedings after the 1969 reforms
(for example, binding over, conditional or absolute discharge, fines, attendance and detention centre orders,
committal to a Crown Court with a view to Borstal training
as well as 'unruly certificates') do not shift central
government responsibility away from the Home Office. With
the exception of the binding over of parents or guardians
and 'unruly certificates', however, all these options were
already available under existing legislation. They were
not new and, in several cases, had already been studied.
Hence the review of this range of 'outcomes' was not part
of our brief either.

In short, we were to examine the operation of those
aspects of Part I of the Act which, chronologically,
affected the progress of young offenders and children in
need of care or protection from the time they first 'came
to notice' to the point at which a decision was made by a

court or other agency about 'what should be done'. This spotlighted a period during which the aim of reducing the number of children coming before the courts would or would not be achieved in practice.

It is noteworthy, of course, that the most radical features of Part I of the Act have, as yet, not been implemented. Section 4, for instance, provides that a person should 'not be charged with an offence, except homicide, by reason of anything done or omitted whilst he was a child'; that is to say anyone under fourteen years of age. But in October 1970 the Government announced that children from ten upwards would remain liable to criminal proceedings; that this age limit might be raised to twelve when the resources of social services departments improved but that it would not be raised any further. Despite changes of government this remains the situation and although care proceedings have become a new option in the case of child offenders the provision has been very little used, as the report from the Expenditure Committee pointed out.

Likewise the most substantial clauses of Section 5 in Part I also failed to be implemented. These place restrictions on criminal proceedings against young people (fourteen and under seventeen) which require that only a 'qualified informant' should 'lay an information' and then not until the appropriate local authority has been consulted. This would have amounted to compulsory consultation prior to the decision to prosecute a young offender. But only the weaker sections 8 and 9 have been implemented; these simply require a person who decides to 'lay an information' to give the local authority notice.

There are other clauses too which still await commencement orders or minister's instructions. There are, for example, clauses in section 7 which allow the minimum age for borstal training to be raised from fifteen to seventeen and which provide for the phasing out of detention and attendance centre orders.

We were, therefore, studying the partial operation of Part I in two senses. First, in as far as it concerned the procedures up to and including a decision about what should be done about 'children in trouble' and, second, with respect only to those sections and clauses which had been implemented by 1 January 1971. These comprised four main changes:

(a) the modification and enlargement of the grounds for care proceedings (section 1), particularly to allow for both offending children and truants to be dealt with under these procedures;

    (b) the replacement of approved school orders and fit
        person orders by a general care order committing
        the child to the care of a local authority;
    (c) the replacement of probation orders for children
        and young persons by supervision orders (with the
        supervisor usually being an officer of the local
        authority but in some cases, where young people
        were involved, it could continue to be a probation
        officer); and
    (d) the requirement that persons laying an information
        (usually the police, but also the NSPCC and educa-
        tion authorities) in either care or criminal pro-
        ceedings inform the local authority of their
        intention. That is, notification became obligatory
        but the consultation voluntary.

GENERAL APPROACH

From the beginning we did not consider that it was possible to undertake an evaluative study of the changes out-
lined above with the resources at our disposal. Comparisons could not easily be made between the old system and
the new, partly because of the difficulty in obtaining
reliable information about what had happened in the past,
and partly because of the numerous other administrative
changes which were occurring concurrently. In particular
there was the Local Authority Social Services Act 1970,
but also the impending major reform of local government.
As a result of such considerations it was agreed to concentrate on describing how Part I of the Act was operating
in selected areas; Bristol and Wiltshire were eventually
chosen.

We also decided to rely primarily upon records for our
source material. From preliminary investigations it
appeared that various records played an important part in
most of the decisions being made about children in
trouble. Clearly other informal communications, especially over the telephone, did influence what was done, but
documentary evidence was assembled and consulted at all
the key stages. In that respect it represented a formid-
able part of the administrative reality which determined
what was remembered, perceived and thought valuable in
coming to decisions.

Other data of a more impressionistic kind might have
been obtained by a participant approach. This would have
offered several advantages. For example, we could have
seen the situations and processes from the standpoint of
those currently involved in them, whether officers,

families or children. It might have been possible, for
instance, to have followed individual children through
from notification to disposition. But this would have
required more time and depended in any case upon obtaining
information from records as a preliminary or supplementary
exercise.

We did, however, feel that it was necessary to gain a
good working knowledge of the main actors and agencies
involved in operating Part I of the Act, not least in
order to understand some of the documentary material which
we used. This led us to undertake relatively unstructured
interviews with the key decision-makers in the system. In
Bristol, these included all the juvenile bureau officers,
all juvenile court chairmen, a random sample of basic
grade probation officers and a similar sample of local
authority social workers. In Wiltshire they included
police officers of various ranks in the three divisions,
juvenile court chairmen for the courts served by full-time
clerks and again random samples of probation officers and
local authority social workers.

In addition we were anxious to see how the juvenile
courts worked in practice, and shorthand records and observations were made for 129 individual cases heard by all
four chairmen in the Bristol court and for 58 cases heard
by all chairmen in the eight Wiltshire courts.

It was harder, however, to decide which basic records
should be used for the main descriptive part of the study.
The problem is that the 'spirit' of the 1969 Act goes
well beyond a narrow definition of children in trouble to
include those 'at risk' of falling into that category.
In this wider sense the 'system' we were to describe
needed to be viewed as embracing all those processes by
which children are prevented from appearing in court.
Clearly some boundaries had to be fixed and careful definitions evolved.

DEFINITION OF THE CHILDREN INVOLVED

Juvenile courts form the nuclei of the system as we con-
ceived it and clearly all children and young persons
appearing before them fell within its ambit. At the
point of a court hearing, and in the procedures associated
with it, various agencies may be involved: the police,
probation, social services departments and the educational
welfare services. Their activities in deciding to bring
the child to court, in providing reports or in giving
evidence are part of this decision system. But, as we
have said, the Act is also concerned with the processes by

which children are not brought to court.

There had to be some way, therefore, of identifying children who came to notice as 'at risk' of appearing before the courts but who had not done so. We hoped that the new social services departments would be in a position to identify an 'at risk' group from amongst the children and young persons known to them. But it soon became evident that, short of launching a separate study on the matter, it would be virtually impossible to distinguish such a group.

A large number of juveniles are known to social services departments but only a minority are likely to be in need of intervention under the terms of the 1969 Act. The point at which a child was easily recognizable as 'at risk' was when a precipitating event or incident actually set in train procedures or activities which were likely to culminate in a court appearance. A small group of care cases in this situation could, for instance, be identified from special lists of children at risk of non-accidental injury. But, at the time, there were no more extensive lists to include children in less extreme circumstances but where, in time, care proceedings might become necessary. Similarly, it was at least as difficult to determine, from existing records, which children were likely to become offenders.

These problems of definition are not confined to social services departments. The education welfare service keep records about a large number of children. Those with attendance problems are relatively easy to identify, yet even amongst them it is hard to decide who runs a substantial risk of being brought to court; non-attendance is dealt with in many other ways as well.

Thus, contrary to our initial assumption, it was not possible to identify children 'at risk' from the general records of the various social work agencies to whom they might be known; at least not without undertaking more preparatory studies than we considered our resources allowed. This led us to the police and their records.

Police records on children differ markedly in at least one respect from those of social work organizations. Since they are much less concerned with general welfare problems most children known to them are (or have been) in situations corresponding to a 'crisis'. Such children comprise those reported for various crimes and summary offences and others who become known for reasons other than the commission of an offence. This later group includes children missing from home, young children found wandering, abandoned or otherwise neglected, as well as some who are involved in domestic disputes. Of

course, not all children known to the police are at risk
of appearing before court but, prima facie, their lists
will contain a much higher proportion of such cases than
those of more general welfare agencies.

The key question, however, is whether in using police
records to obtain an 'at risk' population of children we
exclude a significant number known only to other organizations. We felt fairly sure that on any practical
definition of 'at risk' the great majority of children
and young persons liable to appear before the courts as
offenders would appear in police records. And since, in
most areas, offenders outnumber care cases in court by
some six or seven to one it was at least not unreasonable
to assume a similar, if not exact, relationship between
these groups in any 'at risk' population. Furthermore,
there is consultation between the police and other
agencies about suspected non-accidental injury and, in
Bristol for example, the police often brought care proceedings on behalf of the social services department.
But, in any case, where social services departments bring
children to court as in need of care or protection the
police are usually notified. The only category of children at risk of appearing before the court about whom the
police would rarely have information would be those
involving truancy, although even here they might be
notified.

Such considerations persuaded us to use police records
as the basis for identifying those children who might be
considered to be 'at risk', cross-checked by court
records to be sure that we had included all those who
actually arrived in court.

Thus, in summary, we saw the system to be studied as
embracing those processes associated with decisions made
about any child coming before the courts. Second, and in
addition, we included the processes connected with police
decisions about all children coming to their notice,
whether or not they subsequently came to court. We did
not include the work of the social work agencies unless
it involved children appearing before the juvenile courts
or unless they contributed information to the police or
received information from them. The key bodies in the
study were, therefore, the courts and the police. In our
view a more extensive definition of the system would have
involved a bigger study than our resources permitted.

We did, however, extend the definition in one important
respect: that was to include the British Transport Police.
Their officers have all the powers and duties of police
officers within their particular jurisdictions. To the
casual observer they are indistinguishable from the civil

police and therefore part of this book has been devoted
to a discussion of their work in connection with juveniles
(some 250 children and young people came to their notice
during 1972 in the comparable area of our study).

THE STUDY PERIOD

Our original intention had been to treat the whole of the
year 1972 as the period of our study and draw an appropriate sample. This was far from ideal since the new
arrangements under the 1969 Act would have only operated
for one year. On the other hand it was not practical to
choose a later period or a prospective approach: first
because of the impending reorganization of local authority
boundaries and, second, because the Home Office was keen
to get work under way. The time available to us was
limited.

In the event our plan had to be modified because there
was no baseline of data against which to determine the
accuracy and validity of a sample. We decided, therefore,
to take a census of all children in the system as defined
during the first quarter of 1972 and to make decisions
about the size and type of a subsequent sample for the
remainder of the year from the data thus provided. However, the results discussed in the book, unless otherwise
indicated, refer to the first three months of 1972.

THE ELIGIBLE POPULATION

Eligibility for inclusion in the quarter year census of
1972 was decided by reference to the dates of 'outcome',
rather than by using the dates of first 'coming to
notice'. This, we felt, would be the most convenient way
of specifying the study population (in the event it proved
to be the most difficult). 'Outcome' was defined as the
point at which the child was no longer awaiting a final
decision or result as a consequence of his 'coming to
notice', up to and including a final appearance if he went
to court.

Our decision to include all children and young persons
for whom there was an outcome between 1 January and 31
March 1972 (the whole year was taken in the case of the
BTP) meant that a number were included who first came to
notice towards the end of 1971. Some whose outcomes
occurred after the relevant period, although coming to
notice during that time, were none the less omitted.

The police forces in the study employed the concept of

the 'event' as the unit of their workloads. It seemed
sensible, therefore, for us to make this our basic data
collection unit, thereby preserving information about the
relationships to each other of the various children concerned. This was especially important because a large
number of events involved more than one child. Furthermore, in the case of offences in particular, it was not
uncommon for one event to include a variety of incidents;
as when children went on a shop-lifting spree. It is
sufficient to note here that individual children involved
in these group events were included in the study if, for
them, an outcome had been reached during the relevant
period. This meant that an event might be only partially
incorporated in the study. However, the character of the
whole event was recorded in a summary form, so that it
could be referred to later if necessary.

These various definitions of the study population
provided a total of 1,412 children and young persons in
Bristol and Wiltshire combined for the three month
period, and a further 246 for the whole year who were
known to the railway police.

TABLE A.1   Children and young persons coming to notice
of the police in Bristol and Wiltshire January - March
1972

Offence	Bristol		Wiltshire		Total	
	No.	%	No.	%	No.	%
Offenders	498	63	446	72	944	67
Traffic cases	87	11	103	17	190	13
'Care' cases	185	23	68	11	253	18
Truancy	22	3	3	0	25	2
Total	792	100	620	100	1412	100

Table A.1 shows how the main population is divided by
broad reasons for 'coming to notice'. Overall about two
thirds were notified as offenders; about 1 in 8 for
traffic offences and some 1 in 5 for 'care' or truancy
reasons. Excluding the truancy cases, which are an unrep-
resentative group, two thirds of all these children and
young persons did not eventually appear in court, at
least on this occasion. But the rates differed markedly

between categories; two thirds of traffic offenders went to court; about a third of other offenders but only 1 in 10 of the 'care' cases (see table A.2).

TABLE A.2 Children who went to court

Offence	Bristol			Wiltshire			Total		
	No.	%	As % nos in table A.1	No.	%	As % nos in table A.1	No.	%	As % nos in table A.1
Offenders	150	66	30	156	69	35	306	67	32
Traffic cases	57	25	65	64	28	62	121	27	64
'Care' cases	19	9	10	7	3	10	26	6	10
Total	226	100	29	227	100	37	453	100	32

It is noteworthy that 48 children eventually appeared in other than juvenile courts; that is, almost 11 per cent of all those coming to court. The majority of these cases were heard in magistrates' courts but a small number went on to higher courts.

Notes

Chapter 1   CHILDREN AND THE LAW: 1908-69

1   The Juvenile Court Act, Illinois, 21 April 1899.
2   Mack, The Juvenile Court, 'Harvard Law Review', vol.23, 1909.
3   VII Aethelred 33.
4   Philippe Aries, 'Centuries of Childhood', London, 1962.
5   Treasurer of the Society for the Discharge and Relief of Persons Imprisoned for Small Debts.
6   James Neild, 'State of the Prisons in England and Wales', London, 1812.
7   R. J. Saywell, 'Mary Carpenter of Bristol', Bristol Branch of the Historical Association, Local History Pamphlet, 1964.
8   Anthony M. Platt, 'The Child Savers', Chicago, 1969.
9   Neild, op.cit.
10 The Criminal Law and Prison Reform Committee of the Humanitarian League for example claimed that 'Publicity is the only safeguard against the passing of cruel and excessive birching sentences.' 'Justice of the Peace', 23 May 1908.
11 Herbert Samuel was Under Secretary of State at the Home Office.
12 The Humanitarian League also objected to these powers as 'a dangerous innovation in the case of boys and girls of an advanced age'. Justice of the Peace, op.cit.
13 Herbert Samuel was Home Secretary in 1932.
14 Commons Debate, 12 February 1932, 'Hansard', vol.261, 1180.
15 The Report of the Departmental Committee on the Treatment of Young Offenders, March 1927, Cmnd 2837.

16   The 1948 Children Act, whilst vitally important in other ways, did not significantly affect the operations of the juvenile courts.
17   Section 61, Children and Young Persons Act 1933.
18   Report of the Committee on Children and Young Persons, 196), Cmnd 1191.
19   Children and Young Persons, Scotland, 1964, Cmnd 2306.
20   'Crime - A Challenge To Us All', Labour Party publication, 1964.
21   This account is based on the minutes of the Longford Committee proceedings which are held in the Library of Transport House.
22   'The Child, the Family and the Young Offender', August 1965, Cmnd 2742.
23   National Association of Probation Officers, mimeo, undated.
24   'Children in Trouble', April 1968, Cmnd 3601.
25   Commons debate, 11 March 1969, 'Hansard', vol.779, 1176.
26   Lords debate, 19 July 1969, 'Hansard', vol.302, 1128-.
27   Report of the Committee on Local Authority and Allied Personal Services, July 1968, Cmnd 3703.

Chapter 2   JUSTICE AND WELFARE

1   'Part I of the Children and Young Persons Act 1969. A guide for courts and practitioners', HMSO, 1970.
2   Tove Stang Dahl, The Emergence of the Norwegian Child Welfare Law, mimeo, University of Oslo, 1971.
3   Tadeuz Grygier, 'Juvenile Courts in Europe', mimeo, University of Toronto, 1972.
4   In re Gault. 99. Arizona 180. 1966
5   A survey undertaken by the DHSS Social Work Service during the first months of 1972 estimated that 10 per cent of the time of social services departments was taken up with work with offenders under the 1969 Children and Young Persons Act. DHSS, mimeo, 1972.
6   In practice the contents of social enquiry reports are divulged to defendants or parents at too late a stage in the proceedings and in such a way as to minimize the possibilities of challenge in open court.

Chapter 3   ENTERING THE SYSTEM

1   'Royal Commission on the Police', HMSO, May 1962, Cmnd 1728.

2   E.g., D. J. Bordua, 'The Police: Six Sociological
    Essays', New York, 1967. J. H. Skolnick, 'Justice
    without Trial', New York, 1966. I. Piliavin and S.
    Briar, Police Encounters with Juveniles, 'American
    Journal of Sociology', vol.70, 1964.
3   D. J. Black and A. J. Reiss, Police Control of
    Juveniles, 'American Sociological Revue', vol.35,
    1970. Special Commission on the YDI system of the
    Criminal Justice Co-ordinating Council, Staff-report,
    'Juvenile Record-keeping in New York City', 1971.
    W. F. Hohenstein, Factors Influencing the Police
    Disposition of Juvenile Offenders, 'Delinquency:
    Selected Studies', ed T. Sellin and M. E. Wolfgang,
    New York, 1969.
4   E.g., W. A. Belson, 'The Extent of Stealing by London
    Boys and Some of Its Origins', Survey Research Centre,
    LSE, 1969 and M. Gold, 'Delinquent Behaviour in an
    American City', Belmont, 1970.
5   'Studies in crime and law enforcement in major
    metropolitan areas, Field Surveys I, II and III',
    The President's Commission on Law Enforcement and
    Administration of Justice, 1967.
6   For an account of one such scheme see M. Taylor,
    'Study of the Juvenile Liaison Scheme in West Ham',
    Home Office Research Unit Report, 8, HMSO, 1971.

Chapter 4   CHILDREN IN TROUBLE

1   J. Cowie et al., 'Delinquency in Girls', London, 1968.
    See also M. Felice and D. Offord, Girl Delinquency -
    A Review, 'Corrective Psychiatry and Journal of Social
    Therapy', vol.17, 1972.
2   N. Walker, 'Crime and Punishment in Britain',
    Edinburgh, 1965.
3   E.g., J. F. Short, Jr and F. L. Strodtbeck, 'Group
    Process and Gang Delinquency', Chicago, 1965.
    L. Yablonsky, 'The Violent Gang', New York, 1962.
    A. K. Cohen, 'Delinquent boys: the Culture of the
    Gang', Chicago, 1955.
4   E. H. Sutherland and D. R. Cressey, 'Principles of
    Criminology', Philadelphia, 1955.

Chapter 5   'WITHOUT FAVOUR OR AFFECTION'

1   Commander P. C. Neivens, The Metropolitan Police,
    Juvenile Bureau Scheme, mimeo, undated.

2   Sir Joseph Simpson, KBE, 'Evidence to the Royal Com-
    mission on the Penal System in England and Wales',
    written evidence, vol.IV, HMSO, 1967.
3   J. H. Skolnick, 'Justice without trial', New York,
    1966. I. Piliavin, and S. Briar, Police Encounters
    with Juveniles, 'American Journal of Sociology',
    vol.70, 1964. R. M. Emerson, 'Judging Delinquents',
    Chicago, 1969. A. V. Cicourel, 'The Social Organiz-
    ation of Juvenile Justice', New York, 1968.
4   J. Q. Wilson, 'Varieties of Police Behaviour',
    Cambridge, Mass., 1968.
5   E. Green, 'Judicial Attitudes in Sentencing', London,
    1961. L. T. Wilkins and A. Chandler, Confidence and
    Competence in Decision Making, 'British Journal of
    Crime', vol.5, 1965. D. M. and G. D. Gottfredson,
    Decision Makers Attitudes and Juvenile Detention,
    Journal of Research in Crime and Delinquency',
    July 1969. R. Hood, 'Sentencing the Motoring
    Offender', London, 1972. J. Hogarth, 'Sentencing as
    a Human Process', Toronto, 1971. S. Wheeler, 'Con-
    trolling Delinquents', New York, 1968.
6   M. Grünhut, 'Juvenile Offenders before the Courts',
    Oxford, 1956. N. Goldman, 'The Differential Selec-
    tion of Juvenile Offenders for Court Appearance',
    NCCD, New York, 1963. A. W. McEachern and . Taylor,
    The Disposition of Delinquents, 'Probation Project
    Report I', California, 1966. M. E. Wolfgang, R. M.
    Figlio and T. Sellin, 'Delinquency in a Birth Cohort',
    Chicago, 1972. F. H. McClintock and N. H. Avison,
    'Crime in England and Wales', London, 1968. W. F.
    Hohenstein, Factors Influencing the Police Disposition
    of Juvenile Offenders, 'Delinquency: Selected Studies'
    ed T. Sellin and M. E. Wolfgang, New York, 1969.
    R. M. Terry, 'The Screening of Juvenile Offenders',
    Journal of Criminal Law, Criminology and Police
    Science', vol.58, 1967. D. Steer, 'Police Cautions -
    a Study in the Exercise of Police Discretion', Oxford,
    1970.
7   T. Sellin and M. G. Wolfgang, 'The Measurement of
    Delinquency', New York, 1964.
8   Goldman, op.cit., McEachern, op.cit.
9   T. E. T. Weston, The Alphabet Disorder, 'Medical News',
    1965.
10 C. Bagley, Psychiatric Disorder and Peer Group Rejec-
    tion of the Child's Name, Journal of Child Psychology,
    1970.
11 P. McNaughton-Smith, 'Some Statistical and other Num-
    erical Techniques for Classifying Individuals', HMSO,
    1965.

Chapter 7 'THE INTERESTS OF THE CHILD'

1 See N. Goldman, 'The Differential Selection of Juvenile
   Offenders for Court Appearance', NCDD, New York, 1963.
   A. W. McEachern, The Disposition of Delinquents,
   'Probation Project Report I', California, 1966.
2 'Young Adult Offenders', Report of the Advisory Council
   on the Penal System, HMSO, 1974.

X Priestley and others
s) Children. law.